SETTING THE RECORD STRAIGHT:

American History in BLACK & WHITE

DAVID BARTON

WallBuilder
PRESS

www.wallbuilders.com
Aledo, Texas

Additional materials available from:
WallBuilders
P. O. Box 397
Aledo, TX 76008
(817) 441-6044
www.wallbuilders.com

Cover Painting:
The Granger Collection, New York

Cover Design:
Dennis Gore
Hoyt Communications

Library of Congress Cataloging-in-Publication Data
973.0496073
Barton, David
Setting the Record Straight.
Aledo, TX: WallBuilder Press
192 p; 21 cm.
Bibliography, endnotes and index included.
A transcript of the video and audio by the same title.
E185
ISBN-10: 1-932225-27-7
ISBN-13: 978-1-932225-27-3
1. African American History.   2. African American Politicians.
3. Republican Party.   4. Democratic Party.   I. Title.

Printed in the United States of America

Foreword

African Americans originally came to America unwillingly, having been stolen and sold by Muslim slave-catchers in Africa to Dutch traders journeying to America in 1619. Yet they have withstood those dark beginnings to become the fiber in the fabric of American society. As President William Howard Taft admiringly noted: "Their ancestors came here years ago against their will; and [now] this is their only country and their only flag. They have shown themselves anxious to live for it, and to die for it."

The story of African Americans is not unlike that of God's chosen people, the Jews. Originally prospering in their homeland, they were taken to a foreign land where for centuries they lived in slavery until God delivered them and established them in a new land. Overcoming their tragic beginnings, African Americans have triumphed and prospered – or, in the words of Joseph, whose brethren sold him into slavery: "You intended evil against me, but God turned it for good."

James A. Garfield, America's 20th President, personally witnessed the final chapter in the deliverance of African Americans from slavery in America. He fought to abolish slavery as a Union General during the Civil War and afterwards as a Member of Congress, voted for the abolition of slavery and led in the passage of almost two dozen civil rights bills. Garfield fought side by side with African Americans during the Civil War; and after the War, he worked side by side with America's first African American congressmen to pass those early civil rights bills. President Garfield proudly declared of African Americans: "With unquestioning devotion to the Union – with a patience and gentleness not born of fear – they have 'followed the light as God gave them to see the light.'"

The four-century-long story of African American political history truly is an incredible story but much of the early history is now unknown. That is, while most today know about the last fifty years (i.e., the Rev. Dr. Martin Luther King, Jr., W. E. B. Dubois, and Malcolm X), few know much about the extraordinary heroes from the first three-and-a-half centuries of that history. For example, who today knows the amazing story of the Rev. Hiram Rhodes Revels, the first black U. S. Senator? Or that of Joseph Hayne Rainey, who overcame slavery to become the first African American elected to the U. S. Congress and to serve as Speaker of the U. S. House? Or of John Rock, the first African American admitted to the U. S. Supreme Court Bar? The reintroduction of this history is long overdue.

In speaking of these accomplishments, President John F. Kennedy once observed: "I am certain that it was no easy task to compress into a single volume the American Negro's century-long struggle to win the full promise of our Constitution and Bill of Rights." Such was the case with this work; indeed, it was "no easy task to compress into a single volume" the stories of so many notable heroes, but I have tried.

In the preparation of this work, I have been asked by African American and Anglos alike why I, as an Anglo, would care about the story of African American political history? The answer is simple: it is because I am an American. Period. The story of African American history is part of American history; I am an American, therefore it is part of my history. Furthermore, I am inspired by all stories of sacrifice, courage, and patriotism – regardless of the skin color of the hero. The stories of African American heroes such as Richard Allen, Henry Highland Garnet, and John Roy Lynch are as thrilling to me as are the stories of all other American heroes from Lewis & Clark to Helen Keller to Alvin York.

I hope that you will be as inspired in reading this work as I have been in preparing it.

(I owe a deep debt of thanks to all of those who contributed to this project: Susan Weddington, who first brought to my attention the remarkable history of African Americans in the 1860s and thus launched me on this inquiry; Cheryl, my wife, who has faithfully supported me through thousands of hours of researching, writing, and documenting this work; Nathan Lehman and the research staff who dug through the mountains of dusty archives to resurrect so much of this remarkable but forgotten story; and to God Almighty, for creating us in such a way that we look to, learn from, and are inspired by historical heroes.)

David Barton
December, 2004

Setting the Record Straight:
American History in Black & White

A Primer on African American Political History

African American history – so much of it is truly unknown today. For example, few know of James Armistead – a black patriot and spy who helped make possible the 1781 Yorktown victory during the American Revolution that established America as an independent nation. [1]

Or Peter Salem – a black patriot who was a hero of the 1775 Battle of Bunker Hill; he also fought as one of the legendary Minutemen and was a soldier at the Battles of Saratoga and Stony Point. [2] In fact, a monument was erected to his memory in Massachusetts to commemorate his life and deeds. [3]

And in the famous picture of the 1776 crossing of the Delaware on Christmas night, two men depicted at the front of the boat include Prince Whipple and Oliver Cromwell – two black patriots who served with George Washington and other American generals during the Revolution. [4]

PETER SALEM AT BUNKER HILL   PRINCE WHIPPLE & OLIVER CROMWELL

Few Americans are aware that many of the soldiers who fought during the American Revolution were black – and unlike the later segregated regiments in the Civil War, many of the units in the American Revolution were fully integrated, with black patriots fighting and dying side by side with their white fellow comrades and soldiers. [5]

While this part of our history is unknown today, Americans knew this information in previous generations because of black historians

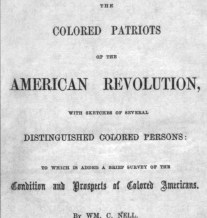

THE

COLORED PATRIOTS

OF THE

AMERICAN REVOLUTION,

WITH SKETCHES OF SEVERAL

DISTINGUISHED COLORED PERSONS:

TO WHICH IS ADDED A BRIEF SURVEY OF THE

Condition and Prospects of Colored Americans.

By WM. C. NELL.

NELL'S 1855 WORK

such as William Nell. Nell was an award winning young scholar in Boston during the 1830s who studied law and became the first black American to hold a post in the federal government. [6] In 1852, he authored *Services of Colored Americans in the Wars of 1776 and 1812*, [7] and three years later he penned *The Colored Patriots of the American Revolution*. [8]

Despite such extensive works, many of our early black heroes and patriots are unknown today; and equally unknown is much of what occurred in black political history. That history will surprise and shock many, but it is a history based on indisputable facts and documents.

Too often, only a handful of the heroes from black history are presented – much like showing only a snapshot or two out of several albums of photos. Too much information is not presented today; and often, too many conclusions are wrongly assumed from the little that is seen.

For example, while students in school early learn that the first load of slaves sailed up the James River in Virginia in 1619 and thus slavery was introduced into America, [9] few learn about the first slaves that arrived in the Massachusetts Colony set up by the Christian Pilgrims and Puritans. When that slave ship arrived in Massachusetts, the ship's officers were arrested and imprisoned and the kidnapped slaves were returned to Africa at the Colony's expense. [10] That side of history is untold today.

THE RELIGIOUS PILGRIMS OPPOSED SLAVERY

A similar omission occurs when the signers of the Declaration of Independence are discussed. For example, if asked to list the slave-owning Founding Fathers among the Signers, no one would hesitate to name Thomas Jefferson. But if asked to name a second slave-owner from among the 56, few other names would be mentioned. And if asked to name the anti-slavery leaders who signed the Declaration, probably no one would mention Samuel Adams – or Stephen Hopkins, or Benjamin Rush, or Elbridge Gerry, or James Wilson, or John Adams, or Roger Sherman, or Benjamin Franklin, or John Witherspoon, or the many other anti-slavery Founders. (To identify these individuals, see illustration on next page.)

Today, black history too often is presented just from a southern viewpoint, describing only slavery and its atrocities as well as the numerous civil rights violations that continued well beyond the end of slavery. Yet there was also what may be called a northern viewpoint, with many praiseworthy events; and to be completely accurate in the telling of black history, the story must be told not only of the martyrs but also of the heroes – just as was done by famous black historians such as William Nell, Carter Woodson, Benjamin Quarles, Joseph Wilson, Booker T. Washington, Edward Johnson, and others. [11]

One of the world's oldest history books – the Bible – offers a good lesson on this point and affirms the approach taken by these black historians. All know the Bible story of David's victory over Goliath, [12] yet the Bible also tells the story of David's adultery with Bathsheba [13] and of his failure with his son Absalom. [14] If only David and his failures

DAVID'S MONUMENTAL VICTORY
OVER THE GIANT GOLIATH

THE PROPHET NATHAN CONFRONTS DAVID
OVER HIS ADULTERY WITH BATHSHEEBA

SIGNERS OF THE DECLARATION OF INDEPENDENCE

1. GEORGE WYTHE, VA
2. WILLIAM WHIPPLE, NH
3. JOSIAH BARTLETT, NH
4. BENJAMIN HARRISON, VA
5. THOMAS LYNCH, SC
6. RICHARD HENRY LEE, VA
7. SAMUEL ADAMS, MA
8. GEORGE CLINTON, NY
9. WILLIAM PACA, MD
10. SAMUEL CHASE, MD
11. LEWIS MORRIS, NY
12. WILLIAM FLOYD, NY
13. ARTHUR MIDDLETON, SC
14. THOMAS HEYWARD, JR., SC
15. CHARLES CARROLL, MD
16. GEORGE WALTON, GA

17. ROBERT MORRIS, PA
18. THOMAS WILLING, PA
19. BENJAMIN RUSH, PA
20. ELBRIDGE GERRY, MA
21. ROBERT TREAT PAINE, MA
22. ABRAHAM CLARK, NJ
23. STEPHEN HOPKINS, RI
24. WILLIAM ELLERY, RI
25. GEORGE CLYMER, PA
26. WILLIAM HOOPER, NC
27. JOSEPH HEWES, NC
28. JAMES WILSON, PA
29. FRANCIS HOPKINSON, NJ
30. JOHN ADAMS, MA
31. ROGER SHERMAN, CT
32. ROBERT LIVINGSTON, NY

33. THOMAS JEFFERSON, VA
34. BENJAMIN FRANKLIN, PA
35. RICHARD STOCKTON, NJ
36. FRANCIS LEWIS, NY
37. JOHN WITHERSPOON, NJ
38. SAMUEL HUNTINGTON, CT
39. WILLIAM WILLIAMS, CT
40. OLIVER WOLCOTT, CT
41. JOHN HANCOCK, MA
42. CHARLES THOMSON, PA
43. GEORGE READ, DE
44. JOHN DICKINSON, PA
45. EDWARD RUTLEDGE, SC
46. THOMAS MCKEAN, DE
47. PHILIP LIVINGSTON, NY

(NOTE: THERE WERE 56 SIGNERS, BUT NOT ALL ARE PICTURED ABOVE)

were mentioned, that would not be the complete story; on the other hand, if only David and his victories were listed, neither would that be the complete story. It takes all sides of a story to see the full, accurate picture. So the Bible (and early writers in black history) illustrate the principle that the good, the bad, and the ugly must be presented in order to transmit the full story not only of history in general but of African American political history in particular – which is the policy that will be pursued in this work. In this chronological journey through many momentous events in black political history, both the people and the issues involved in those early events will be examined.

Although the history of black Americans begins in 1619 with the arrival of the first slaves in America, the *political* history of black Americans actually begins much later, in 1787 – the year in which the American political system was constructed – the year in which the Constitution was written. Today, many  critics assert that the Constitution was a pro-slavery document, and to prove this, they point to the Three-Fifths Clause, claiming that the Constitution says that blacks are only three-fifths of a person. [15]

One of the earliest black Americans to investigate this claim was the famous abolitionist Frederick Douglass. Douglass had been born into slavery and remained a slave until he escaped to New York in 1838. Three years after his escape, he delivered an anti-slavery speech in Massachusetts. He was promptly hired to work for the State's anti-slavery society, and he also served as a preacher at Zion Methodist Church. [16] During the Civil War, Douglass helped recruit the first black regiment to fight for the Union, and he advised Abraham Lincoln on the Emancipation Proclamation

FREDERICK DOUGLASS FLEEING FROM SLAVERY

and other important issues. [17] Following the Civil War, Douglass received Presidential appointments from Republican Presidents Ulysses S. Grant, Rutherford B. Hayes, and James A. Garfield. Democratic President Grover Cleveland removed Frederick Douglass from office but Republican President Benjamin Harrison reappointed him. [18]

WILLIAM LLOYD GARRISON

During Douglass's first years of freedom, he studied at the feet of abolitionist William Lloyd Garrison, who taught him that the Constitution was a pro-slavery document. [19] Douglass accepted this claim, and his early speeches and writings reflected that belief. However, Douglass later began to research the subject for himself; he read the Constitution; he read the writings of those who wrote the Constitution; and what he found revolutionized his thinking. He concluded that the Constitution was not a pro-slavery but an anti-slavery document. [20] He explained:

> I was, on the anti-slavery question, . . . fully committed to [the] doctrine touching the pro-slavery character of the Constitution. . . . I advocated it with pen and tongue, according to the best of my ability. . . . [U]pon a reconsideration of the whole subject, I became convinced . . . that the Constitution of the United States not only contained no guarantees in favor of slavery but, on the contrary, it is in its letter and spirit an anti-slavery instrument, demanding the abolition of slavery as a condition of its own existence as the supreme law of the land. Here was a radical change in my opinions. . . . Brought directly, when I escaped from slavery, into contact with a class of abolitionists regarding the Constitution as a slaveholding instrument, . . . it is not strange that I assumed the Constitution to be just what their interpretation made it. . . . [But] I was [now] conducted to the conclusion that the Constitution of the United States . . . [was not] designed . . . to maintain and perpetuate a system of . . . slavery – especially as not one word can be found in the Constitution to authorize such a belief. [21]

Douglass therefore concluded:

> [T]he Constitution is a glorious liberty document. Read its
> preamble; consider its purposes. Is slavery among them? Is
> it at the gateway? Or is it in the temple? It is neither. . . .
> [I]f the Constitution were intended to be, by its framers and
> adopters, a slaveholding instrument, why neither *slavery*,
> *slaveholding*, nor *slave* can anywhere be found in it? . . . Now,
> take the Constitution according to its plain reading and I defy
> the presentation of a single pro-slavery clause in it. On the
> other hand, it will be found to contain principles and purposes
> entirely hostile to the existence of slavery. [22]

But if the Constitution is not pro-slavery, then what about the
Three-Fifths Clause? Had Douglass not read that clause? Yes, he
had. Then how could he conclude what he did about the Constitution? Douglass understood that the Three-Fifths Clause dealt only
with representation and not the worth of any individual.

The Constitution had established that for every 30,000 inhabitants
in a State, that State would receive one representative to Congress.
[23] The southern States saw this as an opportunity to strengthen
slavery since slaves accounted for much of the southern population
(e.g., almost half the inhabitants of South Carolina were slaves [24]).
Therefore, slave-owners could simply count their slaves as regular
inhabitants, and by so doing could greatly increase the number of
their pro-slavery representatives to Congress.

Of course, the anti-slavery Founders from the North strenuously
objected to this plan. After all, slave-owners did not consider their
slaves to be persons but only property; these slave-owners were therefore using their "property" (that is, their slaves) to increase the power
of the slave States in Congress. The anti-slavery leaders wanted Free
Blacks counted, but not slaves if counting slaves would increase the
power of slave-owners. They understood that the fewer the pro-slavery
representatives to Congress, the sooner slavery could be eradicated
from the nation. Gouverneur Morris – a signer of the Constitution
and a strong opponent of slavery – therefore argued:

GOUVERNEUR MORRIS

Upon what principle is it that the slaves shall be computed in the representation? Are they men? Then make them citizens and let them vote! . . . [But t]he admission of slaves into the representation . . . comes to this: that the inhabitant of Georgia and South Carolina who goes to the coast of Africa and – in defiance of the most sacred laws of humanity – tears away his fellow creatures from their dearest connections and damns them to the most cruel bondage, shall have more votes in a government instituted for protection of the rights of mankind than the citizen of Pennsylvania or New Jersey who views with a laudable [praiseworthy] horror so nefarious [wicked] a practice. [25]

Morris objected to counting slaves because he did not want to reward slave-holders and increase their power. Another ardent anti-slavery delegate at the Constitutional Convention, Luther Martin, similarly explained:

LUTHER MARTIN

[N]o principle can justify taking slaves into computation in apportioning [calculating] the number of representatives a State should have in the government; it involve[s] the absurdity of increasing the power of a State in making laws for freeman in proportion as that State violate[s] the rights of freedom . . . [It] encourage[s] the slave trade and make[s] it the interest of the States to continue that infamous [vile] traffic [so that] slaves could not be taken into account as men or citizens. [26]

Several other Founders – including James Wilson and Elbridge Gerry – even used the slave-holders own arguments against them. [27] For example, Luther Martin, proposed:

> If they [slaves] were to be taken into account as "property," then what peculiar circumstance should render this "property" . . . entitled to the high privilege of conferring consequence and power in the government to its possessors rather than any other property – [that is], why should slaves, as "property," be taken into account rather than horses, cattle, mules, or any other type of property? [28]

These anti-slavery Founders argued that if the South was going to count its "property" (that is, its slaves) in order to get more pro-slavery representation in Congress, then the North would count its "property" (that is, its sheep, cows, and horses) to get more anti-slavery representation in Congress. Of course, the South objected just as strongly to this proposal as the North had objected to counting slaves.

The final compromise was that only sixty percent of slaves – that is, three-fifths of slaves – would be counted to calculate the number of southern representatives to Congress. [29] In other words, it would take 50,000 slaves rather than just 30,000 before slaveholding States could get an additional representative in Congress, thus greatly reducing the number of representatives to Congress from States with extraordinarily large slave populations.

This, then, is the Three-fifths Clause – it had nothing to do with the worth of any individual; in fact, Free Blacks in the North and the South often were extended the full rights of a citizen and regularly voted – both in the North and the South. [30] The Three-Fifths Clause had to do only with representation: it was an anti-slavery provision designed to limit the number of pro-slavery representatives in Congress. [31] This is why Frederick Douglass (unlike many Americans today who have never taken the time to study the Constitution) could therefore emphatically declare that the Constitution – _all_ of the Constitution – was anti-slavery.

In 1789, following the ratification of the Constitution, Congress expanded its fight to end slavery by passing the Northwest Ordinance. That law – establishing how territories could become States in the new United States – forbade slavery in any of the federal territories then held; [32] and for this reason, Ohio, Indiana, Illinois, Iowa, Minnesota, Michigan, and Wisconsin all eventually came into the nation as free States. Even though some slave States were dividing their own State to form new slave States from the old ones – such as Kentucky being formed out of Virginia, or Tennessee from North Carolina – on the federal level, progress was being made toward ending slavery and achieving full civil rights for black Americans.

Another important event in black political history occurred three years later. In 1792 – according to the website of the Democratic National Committee – the Democratic Party was started by Thomas Jefferson. [33] The Democratic Party definitely played a role in black political history – a role that will be examined shortly.

Thomas Jefferson founded the Democratic Party in 1792
MODERN DEMOCRATS CONSIDER JEFFERSON THEIR FOUNDER

In 1808, Congress continued its fight against slavery by abolishing the slave trade. [34] A famous sermon [35] commemorating the abolition of the slave trade was given by the Rev. Absalom Jones, the first black bishop of the Episcopal Church in America. His sermon was delivered in the famous St. Thomas' Church.

St. Thomas' Church – the first black church in Philadelphia – was built in 1792 under the leadership of three famous Americans. One was the Rev. Absalom Jones; another was Dr. Benjamin Rush, a signer

ST. THOMAS' CHURCH

of the Declaration of Independence and a co-founder (along with Benjamin Franklin) of the first abolition society in America; [36] and the third was the Rev. Richard Allen, a famous black minister who regularly preached at a large white mega-church before he started his famous Bethel Church and birthed the AME denomination. [37] These three remarkable Americans helped build the church where this famous sermon on Congress's abolition of the slave trade was preached. That sermon was powerful, and Bishop Jones began it with a Scripture:

EXODUS iii. 7, 8: "And the Lord said, I have surely seen the affliction of My people . . . and have heard their cry by reason of their taskmasters; for I know their sorrows; and I am come down to deliver them." . . .

These words, my brethren, contain a short account of some of the circumstances which preceded the deliverance of the children of Israel from their captivity and bondage . . . They mention, in the first place, their affliction. This consisted in their privation of liberty. . . . Our text

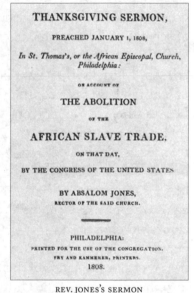

REV. JONES'S SERMON

mentions, in the second place, that in this situation they were not forgotten by the God of their fathers and the Father of the human race. . . . Our text tells us that He saw their affliction and heard their cry. . . . [and was] so much moved with what He saw and what He heard that He . . . [came] down from heaven in His own person in order to deliver them. . . .

[T]he God of heaven and earth is the same yesterday, and to-day, and forever [Hebrews 13:8]. . . . He has seen the affliction of our countrymen with an eye of pity. . . . He has seen the anguish which has taken place when parents have been torn from their

children and children from their parents, and conveyed – with their hands and feet bound in fetters – on board of ships prepared to receive them . . . . He has seen them exposed for sale, like horses and cattle upon the wharves. . . . He has seen the pangs of separation between members of the same family. . . .

[T]hough [masters and mistresses] have been deaf to their cries and shrieks, they have been heard in Heaven. The ears of Jehovah have been constantly open to them:

He has heard the prayers that have ascended from the hearts of His people and He has – as in the case of his ancient and chosen people the Jews – come down to deliver our suffering countrymen from the hands of their oppressors. . . . He came down into the Congress of the United States last winter when they

passed a law, the operation of which commences on this happy day. . . .

[I]n behalf of our brethren, it becomes us this day to offer our united thanks. Let the song of angels, which was first heard in the air at the birth of our Savior [Luke 2:13-14], be heard this day in our assembly. . . . Let us sing psalms unto Him and talk of all His wondrous works. . . . [L]et the first of January – the day of the abolition of the slave trade in our country – be set apart in every year as a day of public thanksgiving . . . . [A]nd when [our children] shall ask in time to come, saying, "What mean the lessons, the psalms, the prayers, and the praises in the worship of this day?", let us answer them by saying, "The Lord – on the day of which this is the anniversary – abolished the trade which dragged your fathers from their native country and sold them as bondmen in . . . America." [38]

Very few today know that in 1808 Congress abolished the slave trade, or that Bishop Absalom Jones delivered such a compelling sermon. Although slavery still had not been abolished in all the States, things definitely were moving in the right direction. Yet a major reversal was about to occur.

By 1820, most of the Founding Fathers were dead and Thomas Jefferson's party (the Democratic Party) had become the majority party in Congress. [39] With this new party in charge, a change in congressional policy emerged.

Recall that the 1789 law prohibited slavery in a federal territory. In 1820, the Democratic Congress passed the Missouri Compromise [40] and reversed that earlier policy, permitting slavery in almost half of the federal territories. Several States were subsequently admitted as slave States; and for the first time since the Declaration of Independence and the Constitution, slavery was being officially promoted by congressional policy. Yet, the only way for the Democratic Congress to promote slavery was to ignore the principles in the founding documents. As Founding Father and President John Quincy Adams explained:

JOHN QUINCY ADAMS

> The first step of the slaveholder to justify by argument the peculiar institutions [of slavery] is to deny the self-evident truths of

the Declaration of Independence. He denies that all men are
created equal. He denies that they have inalienable rights. [41]

Several other pro-slavery laws were also passed by Democrats
in Congress, including the 1850 Fugitive Slave Law. [42] That law
required Northerners to return escaped slaves back into slavery or

else pay huge fines. In many instances,
the law became little more than an excuse
for southern slave-hunters to kidnap Free
Blacks in the North and carry them into
slavery in the South, for if a black was
simply *accused* of being a slave (regardless
of whether he actually was or not), under
the Fugitive Slave Law he was denied the
benefit of both a jury trial and the right of

habeas corpus – despite the fact that those rights had been explicitly
guaranteed by the Constitution.

Because the Fugitive Slave Law became little more than a law to
sanction kidnapping, whenever a slave-hunter entered a State such as
Massachusetts, broadsides were printed to warn black Americans about
this threat to their freedom (e.g., see below: "Proclamation! To all the
good people of Massachusetts! Be it known that there are now three
slave hunters or kidnappers in Boston looking for their prey"). [43] Such
broadsides were published when it was learned that a slave hunter had
come north. The anti-slavery States wanted to make sure that every

POSTERS WERE PRINTED TO WARN BLACKS ABOUT SOUTHERN KIDNAPPERS AND SLAVE HUNTERS

black American in the North could take cover so they would not be kidnapped and taken to slavery in the South.

Because the Fugitive Slave Law allowed Free Blacks to be carried into slavery, this law was disastrous for blacks in the North; and as a consequence of the atrocious provisions of this Democratic law, some 20,000 blacks in the North left the United States and fled to Canada. [44] In fact, the Underground Railroad reached the height of its activity during this period, [45] helping thousands of slaves escape from slavery in the South all the way out of the United States and into Canada – simply to escape the reach of the Democrats' Fugitive Slave Law.

THE UNDERGROUND RAILROAD MOVED THOUSANDS OF BLACK AMERICANS TO SAFETY

In 1854, the Democratically controlled Congress passed another law strengthening slavery: the Kansas-Nebraska Act. [46] Even though Democrats in Congress had already expanded the federal territories in which slavery was permitted through their passage of the Missouri Compromise, they had retained a ban on slavery in the Kansas-Nebraska territory. But through the Kansas-Nebraska Act, Democrats repealed those earlier restrictions, thus allowing slavery to be introduced into parts of the new territory where it previously had been forbidden, thereby increasing the national area in which slavery would be permitted. This law led to what was called "bleeding Kansas," where pro-slavery forces came pouring into that previously slave-free territory and began fighting violent battles against the anti-slavery inhabitants of the territory. [47]

(The term "Kansas-Nebraska Territory" does not describe the area of Kansas and Nebraska as they are known today. In 1854, the Kansas-Nebraska territory included not only Kansas and Nebraska but also what is now part of Colorado, Wyoming, Montana, Idaho, North Dakota and South Dakota. [48] Therefore, by extending slavery into parts of the Kansas-Nebraska territory, Democrats were pushing slavery westward across the nation, essentially from coast to coast.)

THE KANSAS-NEBRASKA TERRITORY COVERED MUCH OF WHAT IS NOW THE UPPER UNITED STATES

Following the passage of these pro-slavery laws in Congress, in May of 1854 a number of the anti-slavery Democrats in Congress – along with some anti-slavery members from other political parties, including the Whigs, Free-Soilers, and Emancipationists – formed a new political party to fight slavery and secure equal civil rights for black Americans. [49] The name of that party? They called it the Republican Party because they wanted to return to the principles of freedom and equality first set forth in the governing documents of the Republic before pro-slavery members of Congress had perverted those original principles. [50]

One of the founders of that new Party was U. S. Senator Charles Sumner, who had taken the seat of the great Senator, Daniel Webster. Sumner had a record of promoting civil rights; in fact, he had championed the desegregation of public schools in Boston [51] and argued on that issue before the State Supreme Court. [52]

Equality before the Law; Unconstitutionality of separate Colored Schools in Massachusetts.

ARGUMENT

OF

CHARLES SUMNER, Esq.,

BEFORE

THE SUPREME COURT OF MASSACHUSETTS,

IN THE

CASE OF SARAH C. ROBERTS vs. THE CITY OF BOSTON,

DECEMBER 4, 1849.

SUMNER'S ANTI-SEGREGATION ARGUMENT
BEFORE THE STATE SUPREME COURT

ANTI-SLAVERY DEMOCRAT CHARLES SUMNER
WAS A FOUNDER OF THE REPUBLICAN PARTY

In 1856, Sumner gave a two-day-long speech in the U. S. Senate against slavery. Following that speech, Democratic Representative Preston Brooks from South Carolina came from the House, across the Rotunda of the Capitol, and over to the Senate where he literally clubbed down Sumner on the floor of the Senate, knocked him unconscious, and beat him almost to death. [53] According to the sources of that day, many Democrats thought that Sumner's clubbing was deserved, and it even amused them. [54] It was three-and-a-half years before Sumner

DEMOCRAT PRESTON BROOKS ATTACKING REPUBLICAN CHARLES SUMNER
FOR SPEAKING AGAINST SLAVERY

recovered his health sufficiently to return to the Senate – and, not surprisingly, the first speech he delivered on his return to the Senate was again against slavery. [55] What happened to Democrat Preston Brooks following his vicious attack on Sumner? He was proclaimed a southern hero and easily re-elected to Congress. [56]

In 1856, the Republican Party entered its first Presidential election, running Republican John C. Fremont against Democrat James Buchanan. In that election, the Republican Party issued its first-ever Party platform. It was a short document with only nine planks in the platform, but significantly, six of the nine planks set forth bold declarations of equality and civil rights for African Americans based on the principles of the Declaration of Independence. [57]

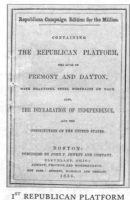

1ST REPUBLICAN PLATFORM

The Democratic platform of that year took an opposite position, strongly defending slavery and warning:

All efforts of the abolitionists . . . are calculated to lead to the most alarming and dangerous consequences and all such efforts have an inevitable tendency to diminish the happiness of the people. [58]

Amazingly, according to Democrats in 1856, ending slavery would not only be dangerous but would also ruin the happiness of the people! Despite such clear differences, the Republicans lost that election.

The next year, 1857, a Democratically controlled Supreme Court delivered the *Dred Scott* decision, [59] declaring that blacks were not persons or citizens but instead were property and therefore had no rights. In fact, quoting from that infamous decision, Democrats on the Court announced that blacks "had no rights which the white man was bound to respect; and that the Negro might justly and lawfully be reduced to slavery for his benefit." [60]

DRED SCOTT

In the 1860 presidential election, Republican Abraham Lincoln ran against Democratic U. S. Senator Stephen Douglas of Illinois. Both parties again issued platforms. The Republican platform of 1860 blasted both the Fugitive Slave Law and the *Dred Scott* decision and announced its continued intent to end slavery and secure equal civil rights for black Americans. [61] On the other hand, the Democrats in their 1860 platform supported both the Fugitive Slave Law and the *Dred Scott* decision. [62] In fact, Democrats even handed out copies of the *Dred Scott* decision along with their platform, to

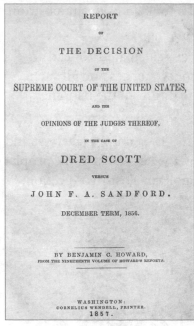

REPORT

OF

THE DECISION

OF THE

SUPREME COURT OF THE UNITED STATES,

AND THE

OPINIONS OF THE JUDGES THEREOF,

IN THE CASE OF

DRED SCOTT

VERSUS

JOHN F. A. SANDFORD.

DECEMBER TERM, 1856.

BY BENJAMIN C. HOWARD,
FROM THE NINETEENTH VOLUME OF HOWARD'S REPORTS.

WASHINGTON:
CORNELIUS WENDELL, PRINTER.
1857.

DEMOCRATS PROUDLY DISTRIBUTED THE
DRED SCOTT RULING WITH THEIR PLATFORM

affirm their belief that it was proper to have slavery and to hold African Americans in bondage. [63]

It is worth noting that for over a century-and-a-half, Democrats often have taken a position that some human life is disposable – as they did in the *Dred Scott* decision. In that instance, a black individual was not a life, it was property; and an individual could do with his property as he wished. Today, Democrats have largely taken that same position on unborn human life – that an unborn human is disposable property to do with as one wishes.

African Americans were the victims of this disposable-property ideology a century-and-a-half ago, and still are today. Consider: although 12 percent of the current population is African American, [64] almost 35 percent of all abortions are performed on African Americans. [65] In fact, over the last decade, for every 100 African American live births, there were 53 abortions of African American babies. [66] Democrats have encouraged this; and although black Americans are solidly pro-life with almost two-thirds opposing abortion on demand, [67] a number of recent votes in Congress reveals that Democrats hold exactly the opposite view, with some 80 percent of congressional Democrats being almost rabidly pro-abortion and consistently voting against protections for innocent unborn human life. [68] For over a century-and-a-half, Democrats have wrongly argued that some human life is merely disposable personal property; black Americans have suffered most under this philosophy.

In the 1860 presidential election, there was a split in the Democratic Party: the northern Democrats and the southern Democrats. Both factions supported slavery; but while southern Democrats were willing to split the United States to form their own nation over the issue, northern Democrats refused to do so. Northern Democrats voted for Stephen Douglas for President while southern Democrats voted for John C. Breckenridge. With this split in the Democratic vote, Republican Abraham Lincoln was elected with only 40 percent of the popular vote, but 59 percent of the Electoral College vote. [69] Republicans also won a majority in the U. S. House and Senate in

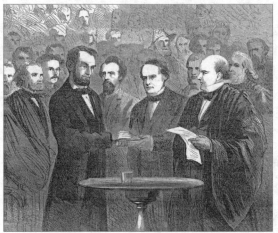

that election, thus giving Republicans control of the lawmaking process for the first time.

Given the bold anti-slavery and pro-civil rights positions set forth by Republicans in their platforms, it was obviously to Democrats what was soon to occur: the anti-slavery and pro-civil rights positions of the

LINCOLN'S INAUGURATION AS PRESIDENT

Republicans were about to become reality. What was the Democrat's response? Southern Democrats left Congress and took their States with them, [70] forming a nation that described itself as the "slaveholding" [71] Confederate States of America. While northern Democrats did not sup-

port this secession, they still supported slavery and opposed civil rights for black Americans. In short, the main difference between southern and northern Democrats at that time was their view on secession, not slavery. [72]

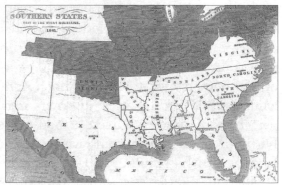

THE SLAVE-HOLDING NATION FORMED BY DEMOCRATS

Regrettably, many Democrats actually rejoiced over Lincoln's election, for it had given them the excuse they wanted to secede and form their slaveholding nation. [73] This was especially true with the Knights of the Golden Circle, an organization composed almost exclusively of Democrats. Before the Civil War, The Knights of the Golden Circle had worked to establish a separate slave nation that included the southern United States, Mexico, and part of Central America. When the Civil War (also called "The War Between the States" or "The Great Rebellion") broke out, these Democrats narrowed their broad goals, focusing instead on making the Confederate States of America a separate slave nation. [74]

Who were the leaders of that new nation of slaveholding States? Democratic U. S. Senator Jefferson Davis of Mississippi resigned from the Senate to become the President of this new slaveholding nation, and Democratic Representative Alexander Stephens of Georgia resigned from the House to become its Vice-President. The

DEMOCRATS JEFFERSON DAVIS AND ALEXANDER STEPHENS LED THE CONFEDERACY

citizens of this new slaveholding nation became known as "Rebels" since they were in rebellion against the United States.

This is not to say that every southern Rebel was a slaveholder or that every Southerner supported slavery, for such definitely was not the case. [75] Yet many modern defenders of the southern Confederacy, in their misguided efforts to prove that slavery was not the primary issue during the Civil War, assert that only 5 percent of Southerners owned slaves. [76] Such numbers are misleading, for while only 5 percent of Southerners may have owned slaves, 19 percent of Southerners lived in households that owned slaves. [77] Furthermore, in several southern States – such as South Carolina, Louisiana, Mississippi, Alabama, and others – almost half the population were slaves. [78] This means that in many of the southern States, almost two thirds of Southerners either were slaves, lived in slave households, or owned slaves; and much of the remaining one-third of Southerners made their living by supplying materials or services to the slave homes or plantations. Therefore, the assertion that only 5 percent of Southerners may have owned slaves does not diminish the fact that slavery was *the* dominant industry in the

SLAVERY WAS *THE* DOMINANT INDUSTRY IN THE SOUTH

southern States. Additionally, despite modern attempts to excuse the South through misleading claims that the conflict did not involve slavery, [79] the secession documents of the States that left the Union – as well as the official documents of the new nation itself – prove otherwise. [80] Consequently, since – according to official documents of the South – slavery was *the* primary distinction between the North and the South, Rebels therefore were fighting for the existence of a slaveholding nation.

While "States' Rights" had been the cry of the southern States before the Civil War, that right had related primarily to the right of States to make their own decisions about slavery. When slavery ended, however, the cry of "States' Rights" was still heard from the former States of the Confederacy, but this time it concerned the right of those States to make their own decisions about whether or not to recognize civil rights for black Americans. The phrase "States' Rights" as related to southern States primarily became an euphemism first for holding blacks in slavery and then for subjecting them to Black Codes, segregation, and institutional discrimination. [81]

Returning to the election of 1860, with Republicans firmly in control of the federal government, they quickly began implementing signifi-

IN 1863, LINCOLN ISSUED THE EMANCIPATION PROCLAMATION

cant changes. In 1862, they abolished slavery in Washington, D. C., [82] and in 1863, the Emancipation Proclamation was issued, [83] freeing all slaves in the southern States in rebellion.

The Emancipation Proclamation was eagerly anticipated; many black Americans gathered in groups around clocks or watches eagerly awaiting the arrival of midnight on December 31, 1862 (the Proclamation was to take effect on the first moment of January 1, 1863). Frederick Douglass was in attendance at one such rally, and when midnight arrived, a celebration erupted and Douglass exclaimed:

> It was one of the most affecting and thrilling occasions I ever witnessed, and a worthy celebration of the first step on the part of the nation in its departure from the thralldom [bondage] of the ages. [84]

FREDERICK DOUGLASS

1864 FREEDMEN'S BILL   1864 MILITARY-PAY BILL

In 1864, following the issuance of the Emancipation Proclamation, several civil rights laws – and laws preparing to facilitate civil rights – were passed by Republicans. [85] One was a bill establishing the Freedmen's Bureau [86] and another equalized pay for soldiers in the military, whether white or black. [87] The Fugitive Slave Law was also repealed that year [88] – over the almost unanimous opposition of the northern Democrats still in Congress. [89]

While Republicans were working to end slavery and secure civil rights, the new nation of southern Democrats was determined to head in an opposite direction. In fact, Confederate Vice-President Alexander Stephens (the Democrat from Georgia) delivered an 1861 speech entitled: "African Slavery: The Corner-Stone of the Southern Confederacy." [90] In that speech, Stephens first correctly acknowledged

AFRICAN SLAVERY,

THE CORNER-STONE OF THE SOUTHERN CONFEDERACY.

A Speech by Hon. Alexander H. Stephens, Vice-President of the Confederate States of America, delivered at the Atheneum, Savannah, March 22, 1861.

DEMOCRAT ALEXANDER STEPHENS' SPEECH AS VICE-PRESIDENT OF THE CONFEDERACY

that the Founding Fathers – even those from the South – had _never_ intended for slavery to remain in America:

The prevailing ideas entertained by him [Thomas Jefferson] and most of the leading statesmen at the time of the formation of the old Constitution were that the enslavement of the African was in violation of the laws of nature – that it was wrong in principle – socially, morally, and politically. It was an evil they knew not well how to deal with, but the general opinion of the men of that day was that – somehow or other, in the order of Providence – the institution would be evanescent [temporary] and pass away. [91]

So what did Vice-President Stephens and the new Confederate nation think about these anti-slavery ideas of the Founding Fathers?

Those ideas, however, were fundamentally wrong. They rested upon the assumption of the equality of races. This was an error. . . . and the idea of a government built upon it. . . . Our new government [the Confederate States of America] is founded upon exactly the opposite idea; its foundations are laid – its cornerstone rests

DEMOCRAT ALEXANDER STEPHENS

– upon the great truth that the Negro is _not_ equal to the white man. That slavery – subordination to the superior [white] race – is his natural and moral condition. This – our new [Confederate] government – is the first in the history of the world based upon this great physical, philosophical, and moral truth. [92] (emphasis added)

There was indeed a clear difference between the philosophy of Republicans and Democrats on the issue of race and racial equality. Southern Democrats had been willing to form an entire nation on the foundation of white supremacy – and there was no doubt that the South was strongly Democratic. As a leading South Carolina Democrat testified during an 1871 congressional hearing:

[A]lmost nine hundred and ninety-nine out of every thousand of the *decent* people of South Carolina belong to the Democratic Party; . . . the Republican Party is composed entirely of the *colored* people. [93] (emphasis added)

When it came time for the presidential election of 1864, southern Democrats were still fighting against the Union; therefore, the presidential candidate for the Democrats that year was a Northern Democrat: Union General George B. McClellan. Although McClellan was actually running for president against his own commander-in-chief, there was a clear difference between the two. In fact, Abraham Lincoln had twice replaced McClellan for failing to obey Lincoln's orders to launch aggressive attacks against the Confederacy. [94]

GEN. GEORGE B. MCCLELLAN

These failures by McClellan to obey Lincoln's wishes are perhaps explained by the fact that this Democratic Union General held opinions about slavery and blacks that were not much better than those of the Democrats in the South against whom he was fighting. For example, when southern slaves escaped from their masters and fled to his Union troops for protection, General McClellan – unlike other Union Generals – originally refused to receive those black refugees; instead, he ordered them back to the South – back to the slave masters from whom they had escaped. [95]

LINCOLN TWICE REPLACED GEN. MCCLELLAN

General McClellan's pro-southern sympathetic behavior was in direct contrast with that of other northern military leaders. One example was Col. Fletcher Webster – son of the anti-slavery statesman Daniel Webster – who organized the 12th Massachusetts, a regiment that adopted the popular abolitionist anthem "John Brown's Body" as its regimental song. [96] That unit saw some of the fiercest action in the War, [97] and Fletcher Webster, leader of that hard-fighting abolitionist unit, gave his own life in the fight against slavery, being shot down at the Second Battle of Bull Run. McClellan was clearly out of step with many other Union military leaders;

ABOLITIONIST MARTYR COL.
FLETCHER WEBSTER

and not surprisingly, the anti-black tone of this northern Democrat shone through in his presidential campaign.

For example, in an 1864 campaign piece for General McClellan, he urged citizens to vote for him because – as he explained – "Our bloody civil war has now lasted nearly four years under the mismanagement of Abraham Lincoln. Nearly one million _white_ men . . . have been sacrificed." [98] Notice another of his complaints: "He [Lincoln] has declared his intention to convert it [the Civil War] into a war for forcible abolition and Negro equality, social

The Presidential Election.

VOTE FOR GENERAL McCLELLAN.

Our bloody civil war has now lasted nearly four years, under the mismanagement of Abraham Lincoln.

Nearly one million of white men and four thousand millions of dollars have been sacrificed.

We were told at the outset, by Mr. Lincoln and by Congress, that the war was to be prosecuted for the purpose of maintaining the Union and the authority of the Constitution as against an armed rebellion, and that accomplished, the war should cease. But instead of conducting it for such a purpose, he has declared his intention to convert it into a war for forcible abolition and negro equality, social and political, and is dragging white men from their homes and their families, and forcing them into his abolition crusade and slaughter pens.

DEMOCRAT MCCLELLAN'S 1864 ELECTION PIECE COMPLAINING ABOUT "NEGRO EQUALITY"

and political." [99] According to McClellan, since _white_ lives were being lost, and since Republicans were seeking both abolition and Negro equality, McClellan argues that he, as a Democrat, should be elected to halt those policies.

Republicans also took clear positions on civil rights issues in that 1864 presidential campaign – positions that, obviously, were opposite to those of the Democrats. And although Republicans had already achieved great progress on civil rights in the few years they had controlled Congress, more was needed. As Republican Frederick Douglass explained:

> [W]e have the [Emancipation] Proclamation of January 1863. It was a vast and glorious step in the right direction. But unhappily, excellent as that paper is – and much as it has accomplished temporarily – it settles nothing. It is still open to decision by courts, canons [agency interpretations], and Congress. [100]

Understanding that something was needed that was more far-reaching than just the Emancipation Proclamation or the various civil rights laws, the 1864 Republican platform therefore called for a constitutional amendment to abolish slavery completely; [101] work was begun in Congress almost immediately on that amendment. That same year, President Lincoln won re-election to a second term.

Resolved, That, as Slavery was the cause, and now constitutes the strength, of this rebellion, and as it must be always and everywhere hostile to the principles of republican government, justice and the national safety demand its utter and complete extirpation from the soil of the republic; and that we uphold and maintain the acts and proclamations by which the Government, in its own defense, has aimed a death-blow at this gigantic evil. We are in favor, furthermore, of such an amendment to the Constitution, to be made by the people in conformity with its provisions, as shall terminate and forever prohibit the existence of Slavery within the limits of the jurisdiction of the United States.

REPUBLICANS ISSUE A CALL FOR THE CONSTITUTIONAL ABOLITION OF SLAVERY

In 1865 the Civil War finally came to a close; the nation of slaveholding States had been defeated. President Lincoln and the black troops of the 29th Connecticut Regiment visited Richmond, the former capital of the

MARCHING INTO RICHMOND

Confederate States of America. An officer in that black regiment recorded the scene:

As the President passed along the street, the colored people waved their handkerchiefs, hats, and bonnets, and expressed their gratitude by shouting repeatedly, "Thank God for His goodness; we have seen His salvation." The white soldiers caught the sound and swelled the numbers, cheering as they marched along. All could see the President, he was so tall. One woman, standing in a doorway as he passed along, shouted, "Thank you, dear Jesus, for this sight of the great conqueror." . . . No wonder tears came to his [President Lincoln's] eyes when he looked on the poor colored people who were once slaves, and heard the blessing uttered from thankful hearts and thanksgiving to God and Jesus. Thousands of colored men in Richmond would have laid down their lives for President Lincoln. [102]

PRESIDENT LINCOLN IN RICHMOND

PRESIDENT LINCOLN WALKING THROUGH RICHMOND, GREETED BY GRATEFUL AFRICAN AMERICANS

Another interesting anecdote about President Lincoln involved a Mrs. Carolyn Johnson of Philadelphia, the African American president of an organization to help soldiers. Mrs. Johnson, who had been a slave, wanted to make a gift and give it to President Lincoln for what he had done for black Americans. A Quaker friend of hers wrote a letter introducing Mrs. Johnson to President Lincoln, who agreed to meet with her. When Mrs. Johnson went to meet the President, she brought her Baptist minister with her because she was terrified to speak for fear of embarrassing herself. Her minister spoke with the President and then turned to Mrs. Johnson and asked if she had anything to say. According to Mrs. Johnson's own account:

> I had not a word to say and I cast my eyes upon the floor, when the fire began to burn within me – and I tell you it was the Spirit. I looked up and said, "Mr. President, I believe God has hewn you out of the rock for this great and mighty purpose; so many have been led away by bribes, by silver, and gold, but you have stood firm because God was with you – and He will be with you if you are faithful unto the end." . . . [To which the President replied], "You must give God the praise, and not man." [103]

Mrs. Johnson then presented President Lincoln a magnificent basket of wax fruit that she personally had made for him.

(In each of these accounts – and hundreds of others – the strong Christian faith of black Americans is apparent. That faith is as active today as it ever was: a number of recent polls show that Christian beliefs are higher among African Americans than among any other ethnic group in the country. [104])

Returning to 1865, while there were numerous celebrations by black Americans and others at the end of the Civil War, even before the war had come to an end, a vote had been held in Congress on the constitutional amendment to abolish slavery – the 13th Amendment. [105] Congress passed that Amendment and a poster was quickly issued to honor the 137 members of Congress who had voted to end slavery. [106]

1865 POSTER SHOWING THE MEMBERS OF CONGRESS WHO VOTED TO ABOLISH SLAVERY

At the time of the vote, there were 118 Republicans in Congress and 82 northern Democrats. Of the 118 Republicans, all 118 voted to abolish slavery; of the 82 Democrats, only 19 voted to end slavery – only 23 percent of Democrats [107] – and those were the northern Democrats!

(On the poster, Abraham Lincoln's face was centered at the bottom. This was significant, for under the Constitution, the President actually has no role in the passage of a constitutional amendment. A constitutional amendment is passed simply with a two-thirds vote of Congress followed by the ratification of three-fourths of the States; no approval of the President is required for any constitutional amendment. But President Lincoln was so pleased with the abolition of slavery that – in a very unusual act – he personally signed the 13th Amendment as a symbolic gesture of his strong support. [108])

When the vote was taken in Congress on the 13th Amendment to abolish slavery, the chambers were packed from wall to wall with expectant observers. After the numbers were counted and it was announced that the amendment had passed, a roar erupted from the

CELEBRATING THE PASSAGE OF THE THIRTEENTH AMENDMENT AND THE END OF SLAVERY

thousands in the chamber; hats were thrown and voices were raised in exuberant cheers. Congress had voted to end slavery! How should something that profound be celebrated?

Members of the House asked that a sermon be preached to commemorate the event. And whom did they ask to preach the sermon? The Rev. Henry Highland Garnet, who became the first African American to speak in the halls of Congress.

REV. HENRY GARNET

(While it might sound strange today to hear that a sermon was preached in the Capitol, it was not at all unusual then. In fact, on December 4, 1800, shortly after Congress first moved into the Capitol building, Congress authorized that on Sundays, the Capitol building would be used for church services. [109] By 1867, the largest church in Washington, D. C., was the one at the U. S. Capitol – 2,000 people a week met there for church. [110] So it was not at all unusual to have sermons and religious services in the Capitol.)

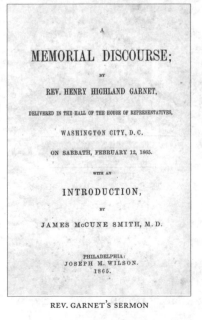

REV. GARNET'S SERMON

Rev. Garnet preached his sermon on Sunday, February 12, 1865, and it was powerful. His discourse began with a recollection of his own personal experiences:

What is slavery? Too well do I know what it is. . . . I was born among the cherished institutions of slavery. My earliest recollections of parents, friends, and the home of my childhood are clouded with its wrongs. The first sight that met my eyes was my Christian mother enslaved. [111]

Garnet then reviewed the prominent historical leaders of both church and state who had strongly opposed slavery:

> Augustine, Constantine, Ignatius, Polycarp, Maximus, and the most illustrious lights of the ancient church denounced the sin of slaveholding. Thomas Jefferson said – at a period of his life when his judgment was matured and his experience was ripe – "There is preparing, I hope, under the auspices of heaven, a way for a total emancipation." The sainted Washington said, near the close of his mortal career and when the light of eternity was beaming upon him, "It is among my first wishes to see some plan adopted by which slavery in this country shall be abolished by law. I know of but one way by which this can be done, and that is by legislative action; and so far as my vote can go, it shall not be wanting." Patrick Henry said, "We should transmit to posterity our abhorrence of slavery." So also thought [this] Congress. . . .

REV. GARNET CITED SEVERAL FOUNDERS WHO HAD CALLED FOR AN END TO SLAVERY

The other day, when the Light of Liberty streamed through this marble pile [building], and the hearts of the noble band of patriotic statesmen leaped for joy, and this our national capitol shook from foundation to dome with the shouts of a ransomed people, then methinks the spirits of Washington, Jefferson, the Jays, the Adamses, and Franklin, and Lafayette, and Giddings, and Lovejoy – and those of all the mighty and glorious dead remembered by history because they were faithful to truth, justice, and liberty – were hovering over the august assembly. Though unseen by mortal eyes, doubtless they joined the angelic choir, and said, "Amen!" [112]

The Rev. Garnet then concluded by calling on the States to ratify the Amendment passed by Congress:

[L]et the verdict of death which has been brought in against slavery by Congress be affirmed and executed by the people. Let the gigantic monster perish. Yes, perish now, and perish forever! . . . Let slavery die. It has had a long and fair trial; God Himself has pleaded against it. Its death warrant is signed by God and man. Do not commute its sentence. Give it no respite [reprieve], but let it be ignominiously executed [put to death with shame and horror]. Honorable Senators and Representatives! Illustrious rulers of this great nation! I cannot refrain this day from invoking upon you, in God's name, the blessings of millions who were ready to perish but to whom a new and better life has been opened by your humanity, justice, and patriotism. You have said, "let the Constitution of the country be so amended that slavery and involuntary servitude shall no longer exist in the United States, except in punish-ment for a crime." Surely, an act so sublime could not escape Divine notice; and doubtless, the deed has been recorded in the archives of Heaven! . . . Favored men – and honored of God as His instruments – speedily finish the work which He has given you to do. *Emancipate! Enfranchise! Educate! and give the blessings of the Gospel to every American citizen!* [113]

This was a momentous event: the first black American to speak in the Capitol – and he delivered a powerful sermon.

Interestingly, at the beginning of this recorded sermon is a reveal-ing message of thanks passed by the leadership of the Rev. Garnet's 15th Street Presbyterian Church in Washington, D. C. The church trustees were so pleased with the honor bestowed on their pastor that they passed a resolution declaring, in part:

Whereas, The Chaplain of the House of Representatives, Rev. Wm. H. Channing, together with a number of the Republican Members of the House, believing that it would be eminently wise and proper to have some public religious service to commemorate such an auspicious event, requested our pastor, Rev. Henry Highland Garnet, to deliver a memorial discourse on the second Sabbath of February, 1865. Therefore

Resolved, That the thanks of the congregation be tendered to those members of the Senate and House of Representatives who voted for said amendment. [114]

Notice in this resolution of thanks that it was the *Republican* Members who had asked Rev. Garnet to speak; the Democrats in the House did not join in inviting him to preach his sermon. Yet

Whereas, The Chaplain of the House of Representatives, Rev. WM. H. CHANNING, together with a number of the Republican members of the House, believing that it would be eminently wise and proper to have some public religious service to commemorate such an auspicious event, requested our pastor, Rev. HENRY HIGHLAND GARNET, to deliver a memorial discourse on the second Sabbath of February, 1865. Therefore

Resolved, That the thanks of the congregation be tendered to those members of the Senate and House of Representatives who voted for said amendment.

THE CHURCH RESOLUTION NOTED THAT IT WAS REPUBLICAN MEMBERS
WHO ASKED THE REV. GARNET TO PREACH HIS SERMON

this is not surprising given the demonstrated attitude of Democrats toward blacks at that time – and it is not surprising considering the Democratic opposition to traditional public religious expressions and activities still demonstrated today.

For example, even though nearly 80 percent of the nation supports voluntary spoken prayer in public schools, [115] only thirteen percent of House Democrats voted for a recent constitutional amendment to permit it (however, 87 percent of Republicans voted for that amendment). [116] And even though almost 80 percent of the nation supports public displays of the Ten Commandments, [117] only 21 percent of Democrats voted for a congressional bill to allow those displays (91 percent of Republicans did so). [118] Consider, too, the congressional bill to remove IRS control from over what pastors can say — a bill that would reinstate freedom of speech to American pulpits exactly the way it had been before Democrat Lyndon Baines Johnson in 1954 had the IRS code amended to restrict speech in churches: [119] only five percent of Democrats voted to allow free speech for churches (but 76 percent of Republicans voted for that bill). [120] And on the vote to protect the Biblical institution of marriage as between one man and one woman,

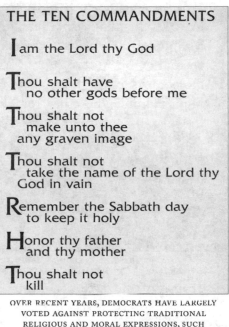

THE TEN COMMANDMENTS

I am the Lord thy God

Thou shalt have
  no other gods before me

Thou shalt not
  make unto thee
  any graven image

Thou shalt not
  take the name of the Lord thy
God in vain

Remember the Sabbath day
  to keep it holy

Honor thy father
  and thy mother

Thou shalt not
  kill

OVER RECENT YEARS, DEMOCRATS HAVE LARGELY VOTED AGAINST PROTECTING TRADITIONAL RELIGIOUS AND MORAL EXPRESSIONS, SUCH AS DISPLAYS OF THE TEN COMMANDMENTS

only 6 percent of Democrats voted to protect that God-ordained institution (88 percent of Republicans did so). [121] There have been many other votes in Congress demonstrating a general Democratic hostility toward laws protecting public religious expressions — similar to their actions a century-and-a-half ago when they would not join in inviting the Rev. Garnet to deliver his sermon.

ATTORNEY JOHN ROCK

At about the same time that the Rev. Garnet preached his sermon, another first in black history occurred. Republican Senator Charles Sumner nominated black attorney John Rock (who also was both a licensed doctor _and_ a licensed dentist) as the first black American to become a member of the U. S. Supreme Court bar; [122] John Rock was then introduced before the U. S. House of Representatives, becoming the first African American attorney to be introduced in Congress. [123]

IN 1865, JOHN ROCK BECAME THE FIRST AFRICAN AMERICAN
TO BECOME A MEMBER OF THE SUPREME COURT BAR

Because of the 13th Amendment and the end of slavery, black Americans – particularly in the South – could now enjoy their first real taste of civil rights – their first genuine opportunity for political participation. Within a year, blacks were registering to vote and were

forming political parties across the South. For example, at a rally in Houston, Texas, on July 4th, 1867, 150 blacks and 20 whites formed the Republican Party of Texas; [124] and black Americans also started other southern Republican parties as well. [125]

ACROSS THE SOUTH, BLACKS REGISTERED TO VOTE
AND FORMED POLITICAL PARTIES

In the years immediately following the Civil War, the former Rebels (who had been almost exclusively Democrats [126]) were not allowed to vote in their States until they took an oath of loyalty. [127] In that oath, they swore first, an oath of allegiance to the United States, and second, an oath to respect the civil rights of black Americans. [128] If a Rebel did not swear this oath, he could not vote – and many Democrats could not vote because they refused to take the oath, or because they could

AMNESTY OATH.

I do solemnly swear or affirm, in the presence of Almighty God, that I will henceforth faithfully defend the Constitution of the United States, and the Union of States thereunder, and that I will in like manner abide by and faithfully support all Laws and Proclamations which have been made during the existing rebellion, with reference to the emancipation of slaves.

SO HELP ME GOD.

Sworn to and Subscribed before me, this

day of _____ A. D., 186_

Clerk of the _____ Judicial District, in and for the Parish of _____

SOUTHERN PRO-SLAVERY DEMOCRATS WERE REQUIRED TO SIGN THIS OATH BEFORE THEY COULD VOTE

not pass other federal requirements. [129] Therefore, for a few years Republicans became the political majority in most of the southern States. Those Republican legislatures moved quickly to protect voting rights for African Americans, prohibit segregation, establish public education, and to open public transportation, State police, schools, and other institutions to black Americans. [130]

Not only were the southern legislatures at that time Republican but (at least for a few years) nearly every southern legislature included many black legislators. In fact, the first 42 blacks elected to the State legislature in Texas were all Republicans. [131] And in Louisiana, the first 95 black representatives and the first 32 black senators were Republicans. [132] Similarly, in Alabama, the first 103 blacks elected to the State legislature were Republicans; [133] in Mississippi, the first 112; [134] in South Carolina, the first 190; [135] in

REPUBLICAN CIVIL RIGHTS LAWS OPENED NEW OPPORTUNITIES TO BLACK AMERICANS

Virginia, the first 46; [136] in Florida, the first 30, [137] and the same in North Carolina; [138] and in Georgia, 41 blacks were elected to the State legislature – all as Republicans. [139]

Of course, Democrats were not pleased with this progress and therefore took decisive action. For example, in Georgia, where the State legislature was still in the hands of Democrats, they ruled

SOME OF THE BLACK REPUBLICAN MEMBERS OF THE LOUISIANA LEGISLATURE

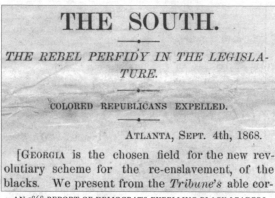

THE SOUTH.

*THE REBEL PERFIDY IN THE LEGISLA-
TURE.*

COLORED REPUBLICANS EXPELLED.

ATLANTA, SEPT. 4th, 1868.

[GEORGIA is the chosen field for the new rev-
olutiary scheme for the re-enslavement, of the
blacks. We present from the *Tribune's* able cor-

AN 1868 REPORT OF DEMOCRATS EXPELLING BLACK LEADERS

that while blacks might have the right to be elected, they did not have the right to serve in office; [140] Democrats therefore expelled 31 elected blacks from the Georgia legislature, thus keeping the majority in the hands of Democrats. [141]

So great were the gains of blacks through the Republican Party that Democrats began to fight back not only as they had in Georgia through the manipulation of laws and election results, but also literally – as in Louisiana. Recall that black Americans had made huge gains in Louisiana with the election of 127 black legislators and even a black lieutenant governor, P. B. S. Pinchback, who later served as State governor. [142] To halt such progress, in 1866, Democrats – in conjunction with the city police and the Democratic mayor of New Orleans – physically attacked the Republican Convention in that city, killing 40 blacks, 20 whites, and wounding 150 others. [143] Democrats later (in 1875) rushed the floor of the Louisiana Legislature to seize power – by force – away from the elected black Republicans, but federal troops arrived to restore

P.B.S. PINCHBACK

peace and return African Americans to their lawfully elected positions. [144] Similar violent and often deadly attacks by Democrats against Republicans also occurred in other States. [145]

While much early Democratic opposition occurred on a State by State or local basis, in 1866 Democrats formed a group that became

DEMOCRATS ATTACKED AND KILLED BOTH
BLACK AND WHITE REPUBLICANS

DEMOCRATS RUSHED THE LEGISLATURE
TO EXPEL BLACK REPUBLICANS

national. Its declared purpose was to break down the Republican government and pave the way for Democrats to regain control in the elections. What was the name of that group? The Ku Klux Klan. [146]

1872 CONGRESSIONAL DOCUMENTS IRREFUTABLY PROVE THAT
DEMOCRATS STARTED THE KU KLUX KLAN

Although it is relatively unreported today, historical documents
are unequivocal that the Klan was established by Democrats and that
the Klan played a prominent role in the Democratic Party. [147] In fact,
a thirteen-volume set of congressional investigations from 1872 [148]
conclusively and irrefutably documents that fact. [149] Contributing
to the evidences was the 1871 appearance before Congress of leading
South Carolina Democrat E. W. Seibels who testified that "they [the
Ku Klux Klan] belong to the reform party – [that is, to] our party,
the Democratic Party." [150]

The Klan terrorized black Americans through murders and
public floggings; relief was granted only if individuals promised
not to vote for Republican tickets, and violation of this oath was
punishable by death. [151] Since the Klan targeted Republicans in
general, it did not limit its violence simply to black Republicans;
white Republicans were also included. [152] In 1871, Joseph Hayne
Rainey, a black U. S. Congressman from South Carolina, reported

THE KLAN HUNG REPUBLICANS, WHITE AS WELL AS BLACK

an incident concerning an elderly man named Dr. John Winsmith, a white Republican State Senator:

The doctor, a man nearly seventy years of age, had been to town during the day and was seen and talked with by many of our citizens. Returning home late, he soon afterward retired, worn out and exhausted by the labors of the day. A little after midnight he was aroused by someone knocking violently at his front door.... The doctor arose, opened the door, and saw two men in disguise standing before him. . . . The doctor immediately stepped back into the room, picked up two single-barreled pistols lying upon the bureau, and returned to the open door. At his reappearance the men retreated behind some cedar trees standing in the yard. The doctor, in his night clothes, boldly stepped out into the yard and followed them .... He continued to advance, when twenty or thirty shots were fired at him by men crouched behind an orange hedge. He fired his remaining pistol and then attempted to return to the house. Before reaching it, however, he sank upon the ground exhausted by the loss of blood and pain, occasioned by seven wounds which he had received in various parts of his body. As soon as he fell, the assassins mounted their horses and rode away... He [had] joined the Republican Party in the fall of 1870; and for this alliance – and this alone – he has been vehemently assailed and murderously assaulted. . . . Because he has dared become a Republican, . . . he has become the doomed victim of the murderous Ku Klux Klan. [153]

REPUBLICAN U.S. REP. JOSEPH H. RAINEY

The Klan shot down this white State Senator because he was Republican and was fighting for the rights of blacks in his State. Even though Dr. Winsmith was hit seven times in that hail of bullets, he survived the shooting and lived to testify before Congress about the attack made on him by the Klan. [154]

In 1868, the Klan in South Carolina issued a push-card about the size of a baseball card. [155] It pictured 63 "Radicals"; they were all Republicans. (The Democrats called Republicans "radicals" because the Republican Party was bi-racial and allowed blacks to vote and to participate in the political process, [156] thus making them "radical" in the eyes of Democrats.) Of the 63 "Radicals" – or Republicans – in the South Carolina legislature, 50 were black and 13 white.

RADICAL MEMBERS
OF THE So. CA. LEGISLATURE.

KKK CARD IDENTIFYING REPUBLICANS IN THE SOUTH CAROLINA LEGISLATURE: 50 BLACKS AND 13 WHITES

On the back of the card, all the names of the Republicans were listed; evidently, if the Klan wanted to pay them a night visit – as they had to Senator Winsmith – with the help of this card, they would know exactly for whom they were looking.

Although much progress had been made because of the 13th Amendment and the civil rights laws passed in Congress, Democrats in the South still found ways to ignore those laws. Although forced to acknowledge that slaves had become free, they denied former slaves the rights of citizenship in those States, therefore withholding from them the rights accorded to all other citizens in their State. Congress responded with the 14th Amendment – a civil rights amendment to the Constitution declaring that former slaves were full citizens of the State in which they lived and were therefore entitled to _all_ the rights and privileges of any other citizen in that State.

When the 14th Amendment came to a vote, 94 percent of the Republicans in Congress voted for the passage of that civil rights Amendment; however, the records of Congress reveal that not one Democrat – either in the House or the Senate – voted for the 14th Amendment! [157] Three years after the Civil War, and Democrats from the North as well as the South were still refusing to recognize _any_ rights of citizenship for black Americans!

Perhaps this lack of support for civil rights is not surprising considering the makeup of the national Democratic Party at that time. A handbill highlighting some of the distinguished notables at the 1868 Democratic National Convention held in New York City on July 4th of that year reveals that Democratic delegates to that Convention included:

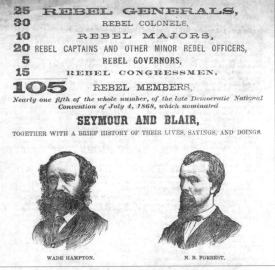

DELEGATES TO THE 1868 DEMOCRATIC NATIONAL CONVENTION

Rebel Generals (25), Rebel Colonels (30), Rebel Majors (10), Rebel Captains and other Minor Rebel Officers (20), Rebel Governors (5), Rebel Congressmen (15), [and therefore a total of] Rebel Members (105). [158]

THE 1868 DEMOCRATIC NATIONAL CONVENTION

Nearly one-fifth of the members of the Democratic National Convention were leaders who had either militarily fought for or politically led the slaveholding nation in the South. The handbill also featured portraits of two prominent Rebel Generals who participated in that Convention.

One was Wade Hampton. Before the war, Hampton had been a Democratic U. S. Senator from South Carolina, but he vacated the Senate to join the new slaveholding nation formed by southern Democrats. In 1876, Hampton ran for the Democratic governorship of South Carolina; one of his active allies in that election was a group called

GEN. WADE HAMPTON the "Red Shirts," [159] which was essentially the Klan dressed in red shirts rather than white hoods. To help win Hampton's governor's race, they issued the following guidelines:

> Every Democrat must feel honor bound to control the vote of at least one Negro by intimidation, purchase, keeping him away, or as each individual may determine how he may best accomplish it. We must attend every Radical [i.e., Republican] meeting that we hear of, whether they meet at night or in the daytime. Democrats must go in as large numbers as they can get together – and well-armed. [160]

"OF COURSE HE WANTS TO VOTE THE DEMOCRATIC TICKET!"

HOW DEMOCRATS CONVINCED BLACK VOTERS NOT TO VOTE REPUBLICAN

Leading newspapers of the day – such as *Harper's Weekly* – included an illustration demonstrating how Democrats controlled votes in those elections (see illustration on previous page). [161] In fact, during a congressional hearing about whether southern blacks voted Democrat, the following exchange occurred:

Q. Were there many colored Democrats there?

A. Very few indeed; some barbers and a few men that worked in towns *pretended* to be Democrats.

Q. Do you know any colored men who were Democrats from instinct?

A. No sir; only from the instinct of self-preservation. [162]

Even with the massive voter intimidation in Wade Hampton's election, it was still so close that no winner emerged. After massive controversy, confusion, and finally court intervention, the Democrat Hampton was declared the winner and became governor, but only under extremely questionable circumstances. [163] In fact, the editorial cartoons in *Harper's* following that election showed a triumphant Democrat standing over the bodies of slaughtered African American voters. [164] Considering the Klan-like support that Hampton received,

THE "BLOODY SHIRT" REFORMED.

Harper's Weekly

it is no wonder that when he became the Democratic governor of the State, civil rights reforms in South Carolina came to a halt. [165]

However, returning to General Hampton's role at the Democratic National Convention of 1868, as a member of the Resolutions Committee, he inserted a clause in the Democratic platform declaring that the civil rights laws of the Congress were "unconstitutional, revolutionary, and void." [166] In fact, throughout that platform Democrats lashed out against the Republican civil rights measures, demanding "the abolition of the Freedmen's Bureau and all political instrumentalities designed to secure Negro supremacy." [167] That platform further complained:

> Instead of restoring the Union, it [the Republican Party] has – so far as in its power – dissolved it, and subjected ten States, in time of profound peace, to military despotism and Negro supremacy. [168]

Clearly, the errant claims in this Democratic plank are ludicrous, for the years from 1865-1868 were marked not by "profound peace" but rather by profound violence, characterized by the rapid and expansive growth of the Klan and similar organizations perpetrating numerous deadly attacks against African Americans. The ten States that Democrats claim were "subjected to military despotism and Negro supremacy" were ten of the Democratic States that had seceded to form the slave-holding Confederate States of America, and the "despotism" to which they were subjected was nothing more than the requirements that they recognize the civil rights of African Americans. Ironically, Democrats were so accustomed to the suppression of black Americans that simply to give them equality was absurdly considered to be "Negro supremacy." To Democrats in that day, equality for blacks – that is, making blacks and whites equal before the law – meant "Negro supremacy"!

The other featured portrait in the handbill of the 1868 national Democratic delegates was that of Rebel General Nathan Bedford Forrest. Forrest had been a slave-trader from

GEN. NATHAN
BEDFORD FORREST

Tennessee and was the Rebel General who conducted the massacre of black soldiers in the infamous bloody episode at Fort Pillow. After the black Union soldiers had surrendered, Forrest ordered them slaughtered on the spot, using some of the most barbaric and inhumane tortures and atrocities available, including nailing black soldiers to the sides of buildings and then burning down the buildings, drowning others, and even burying black soldiers alive. [169] After

GEN. NATHAN BEDFORD FORREST LED THE SLAUGHTER OF AFRICAN AMERICANS AT FORT PILLOW

the War, General Nathan Bedford Forrest became the first Grand Wizard of the Ku Klux Klan [170] – and he was an honored leader at the Democratic National Convention of 1868! Given the composition of the Democratic Party, it is no wonder that not one of the Democrats in Congress voted for the 14th Amendment to secure civil rights for black Americans at the State level.

Even though huge steps in obtaining civil rights had been achieved through the 13th and the 14th Amendments (as well as through several federal civil rights laws), the staunch and steadfast resistance of the southern Democratic States to those measures continued; they simply ignored the constitutional Amendments and the federal laws. [171] Congress therefore imposed requirements that before the former Confederate States could be readmitted into the United States, they must first approve both the 13th and 14th Amendments, [172] and

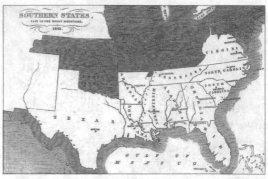

THE SOUTHERN STATES WERE REQUIRED TO RECOGNIZE CIVIL RIGHTS BEFORE BEING READMITTED TO THE UNITED STATES

then must create new state constitutions that guaranteed equal civil rights for black Americans. [173]

As a result of those requirements, Alabama rewrote its constitution in 1867; in 1868, Arkansas, Florida, Georgia, Louisiana, Mississippi, North Carolina, South Carolina, and Texas rewrote their constitutions; and in 1870, Tennessee and Virginia became the last of the former Confederate States to rewrite their State constitutions. However, the votes to ratify these new constitutions granting civil rights to black Americans were met with massive resistance and widespread riots and attacks by Democrats throughout those States.

DEMOCRATS ATTACKED AFRICAN AMERICANS TO PREVENT THEM FROM VOTING

For example, in 1868 in Mississippi, Democrats and the Klan attacked blacks on their way to vote for the new constitution, [174] and the Republican officials administering those elections were similarly attacked. [175] Former State Governor William Sharkey – appointed by Democratic President Andrew Johnson – led an armed band that attacked and threatened election officials. [176] Order was not restored until federal troops arrived to quell what one official committee described as the Democrats' "reign of terror." [177]

As a result of the events in Mississippi, the congressional Committee on Reconstruction convened extensive hearings. [178] For those who have heard so little of this part of American history – or especially of this part of African American political history – the hearings provided what today's citizens might consider shocking informa-

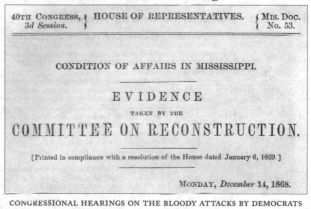

CONGRESSIONAL HEARINGS ON THE BLOODY ATTACKS BY DEMOCRATS

tion. Consider, for example, the testimony of election worker Robert Flournoy, given before the Committee on December 15, 1868:

Q: How long have you resided in Mississippi?

A. Twelve years. I was born in Georgia.

Q. What means have you had within the last year of knowing the sentiment of the people of Mississippi concerning the constitution that was framed by the convention?

A. I canvassed a large portion of the State in favor of the adoption and ratification of the constitution. . . . Of course I made it my business to ascertain the sentiment of the people from what I could judge in the general expressions of approval or disapproval of remarks made; and I took it upon myself to converse freely with the people. I am a considerable sort of a

Negro man and talk with the Negroes wherever I go. I have
never met in all my [interaction] with the Negroes of Mississippi but one single Negro who professed to be a Democrat,
and that was in the town of Oxford. He was a waiter in a
hotel, and he informed me that he was a Democrat. I tried to
convert him and failed, and left him a Democrat. [179]

This election official could find only one black American in the
entire State of Mississippi who was a Democrat!

Significantly, in Mississippi at that time, there were 444,000 blacks
and only 383,000 whites; [180] and since blacks voted overwhelmingly
Republican, only by preventing them from voting could Democrats
defeat the new State constitution with its civil rights provisions – hence
the cause of the violence. In fact, a newspaper illustration from that
time shows a murdered African American with KKK etched on the
wall above him and the caption "One Vote Less," [181] demonstrating
the declaration of Colonel French Smith at a Democratic convention in Texas in which he declared, "I love to kill Indians, but would
rather kill one Negro than two Indians!" [182]

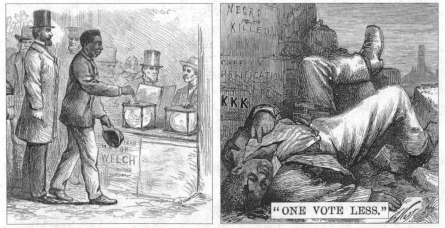

ONE OF THE WAYS THAT DEMOCRATS KEPT AFRICAN AMERICANS FROM VOTING REPUBLICAN

Despite this strident opposition throughout the southern States,
the new constitutions were eventually passed and a number of black
Americans were elected to national office. An 1872 print by Currier

and Ives showed the first seven black Americans elected to the U. S. Congress [183] – all were Republicans.

THE FIRST SEVEN AFRICAN AMERICANS ELECTED TO THE U. S. CONGRESS – ALL REPUBLICANS

On the left side of that group was Hiram Rhodes Revels from Mississippi. An ordained minister, he served as a missionary and pastor, recruited three black regiments, and was a chaplain during the Civil War. Revels became America's first black U. S. Senator. [184]

Next was Benjamin Turner of Alabama. Turner was a slave during the Civil War but within five years after the war had become a wealthy and prosperous businessman. [185]

Third was Robert De Large of South Carolina. Born as a slave,

REV. REVELS RECRUITED THREE BLACK REGIMENTS

within three years from the end of the War he was serving in the State House; he also chaired the Republican Party's Platform Committee and became a statewide elected official. [186]

Fourth was Josiah Walls of Florida. Walls was a slave during the Civil War and was forced to fight for the Confederate Army; after he was captured by Union troops, he promptly enlisted as a Union soldier and became an officer. Following his election to Congress, his credentials were challenged by Democrats and he was twice sent home. He was re-elected after the first challenge, but during the second challenge, Democrats regained control of Florida and he was prevented from returning. [187]

Fifth was Jefferson Long of Georgia. Born as a slave, he was self-educated and built a thriving business. However, when elected to Congress as a Republican, Democrats boycotted his business, causing him great financial losses. Long was the first black American to deliver a congressional speech in the U. S. House. [188]

Sixth was Joseph Hayne Rainey of South Carolina. Born a slave, he actually served briefly as Speaker of the U. S. House and was in Congress longer than any other black American from that era. [189]

The seventh was Robert Brown Elliott, also of South Carolina. He was well educated, reading in Spanish, French, and Latin. In Congress, he led in the passage of civil rights bills over the strident opposition of congressional Democrats; he later became Speaker of the House in the State legislature. [190]

Just as they had with Rep. Josiah Walls, Democrats in Congress regularly challenged the credentials of black Americans, attempting to have them expelled from Congress on technical or procedural grounds. An 1870 Cleveland newspaper described the attempt by the Democrats to prevent the seating of Hiram Rhodes Revels as the nation's first black Senator:

> [T]he business relative to the credentials of Mr. Revels as Senator from Mississippi was taken up. The debate which followed assumed a wide range of political questions. At 4:40 o'clock, a vote was taken upon the motion of Mr. Stockton [a

Democratic Senator from New Jersey] to refer the credentials of Mr. Revels to the judiciary committee. [191]

Democratic Senator Stockton was alleging that Revels did not have proper credentials to serve as a U. S. Senator and therefore wanted the Senate Committee to investigate in order to delay or prevent Revels from being seated. What was the result of this attempt?

NEWSPAPER DESCRIBING THE SWEARING IN OF SEN. REVELS

> Defeated by a party vote – yeas 8, nays 48. The vote to administer the oath resulted – 48-8. [192]

All 48 Republicans said that Revels had the right to serve in the Senate; all 8 Democrats said he did not. Once the credentials of Revels had been established:

> Mr. Revels was then conducted in front of the President's desk by Mr. Wilson [a leading Republican Senator], the oath administered, and he entered upon his office. Mr. Revels took the seat assigned to him, on the Republican side, where a number of Senators and others tendered him congratulations. [193]

Revels took the seat once held by U. S. Senator Jefferson Davis of Mississippi, who left the Senate in 1861 and became the President of the slaveholding Confederate States of America. The newspapers of the day did not fail to note the irony that a black Republican Senator had taken the same seat once held by racist Democrat [194] Jefferson Davis. [195] In the illustration from *Harper's Weekly*, the Republicans were gathered around Senator Revels, but skulking in the foreground was Democrat Jefferson Davis, filled with rage and hatred as a black Republican takes his seat.

RACIST DEMOCRATIC SENATOR JEFFERSON DAVIS FILLED WITH RAGE
AS BLACK REPUBLICAN SENATOR HIRAM REVELS TAKES HIS SEAT IN THE SENATE

Shortly after the seating of Revels, the question arose: should
Georgia should be permitted to have representation in Congress
– was the State "reconstructed" enough in its attitudes toward

black Americans to receive a seat at the federal table once again? Senator Revels strongly supported the readmission of Georgia, knowing that allowing it back into Congress would mean that the newly freed blacks in Georgia would have a voice at the federal level. In that speech – his very first in the Senate – Revels declared:

> [I] lift my voice for the first time in this Council Chamber of the nation; and, sir, I stand today on this floor to appeal for protection from the strong arm of the government for her loyal children – irrespective of color and race – who are citizens of the southern States and particularly

REPUBLICAN SENATOR HIRAM R. REVELS, AMERICA'S FIRST BLACK U. S. SENATOR

> the State of Georgia. . . . [The] race which the nation raised from the degradation of slavery and endowed with the full and unqualified rights and privileges of citizenship. . . . ask but the rights which are theirs by God's universal law. . . . And here let me say further, that the people of the North owe to the colored race a deep obligation which it is no easy matter to fulfill. When the

> federal armies were thinned by death and disaster. . . . from what source did our nation – in its seeming death throes – gain additional and new-found power? It was the sable [black]

> sons of the South that valiantly rushed to the rescue; and but for their intrepidity [bold courage] and ardent daring, many a northern fireside would miss today paternal counsels or a

brother's love. . . . Many of my race . . . sleep in the countless graves of the South. . . . And now, sir, I protest in the name of truth and human rights against any and every attempt to fetter the hands of one hundred thousand white and colored citizens of the State of Georgia. . . . I wish my last words upon the great issues involved in the bill before us to be my solemn and earnest demand for full and prompt protection for the helpless loyal people of Georgia. [196]

Georgia was readmitted. [197]

While the Rev. Hiram Rhodes Revels was the first black American to serve in the U. S. Senate, there have been others as well. The second

was Blanche Kelso Bruce of Missis-sippi – the first to serve a full term in the Senate. Bruce also received an ap-pointment to a federal post by Repub-lican President James A. Garfield; [198] a portrait of Senator Bruce today hangs on the Senate side of the U. S. Capitol. The third black Senator was Edward Brooke of Massachusetts who was the first to be elected in a statewide vote. [199] (Prior to the adoption of the 17th Amendment to the Constitution in 1913, the U. S. Senators for a State were chosen by the State legislature, and

REPUBLICAN SENATOR BLANCHE K. BRUCE, AMERICA'S SECOND BLACK U. S. SENATOR

both Revels and Bruce were chosen in this manner; however, Edward Brooke was the first black Senator chosen by the people in a statewide election.) Significantly, the first three black U. S. Senators – Revels, Bruce, and Brooke – were all Republicans. Carol Moseley-Braun (of Illinois) was the fourth black American to serve in the U. S. Senate, but only the first Democrat; and Barack Obama (also from Illinois) was only the second black Democratic U. S. Senator.

The first African American elected to the U. S. House was Joseph Hayne Rainey of South Carolina. [200] Rainey was the first of twenty-three black Americans elected to the U. S. Congress [201] – all as Republicans. Remarkably, of those early black Congressmen, thirteen had been slaves [202] (consider the amazing transformation that this represents: in only five years, black Americans had gone from being slaves to becoming Members of Congress!), and all of them were home or self-educated. Additionally, three of that group were ministers, seven were attorneys, five were schoolteachers, four were university presidents, and thirteen were state legislators [203] – a distinguished group with momentous achievements.

Democrats did not elect their first black American to the U. S. House until 1935, [204] and that black Member was from Illinois – a northern State in which blacks had always been free. It was not until 1973 that the first black Americans from the South were elected to Congress as Democrats: Barbara Jordan of Texas and Andrew Young of Georgia – and they were elected only after the U. S. Supreme Court struck down the gerrymandered district lines that southern Democratic State legislatures had drawn that kept blacks from being elected. [205]

While black Americans immediately following the Civil War had indeed begun a distinguished chapter in their history, the opposition to their rapid success grew just as rapidly. Many southern Democrats not only despised blacks and Republicans but they utilized every means possible to keep them from voting – including not only the use of devious and cunning means but also the direct use of violence. In fact, after examining the abundant evidence concerning this violence, U. S. Senator Roscoe Conkling (nominated as a U. S. Supreme Court Justice) concluded that the Democratic Party was determined to exterminate blacks in those States where Democratic supremacy was threatened. [206] As a response to Democratic violence in the South, and in order to further secure the civil rights of black Ameri-

DEMOCRATS LYNCHED A BLACK AND A WHITE REPUBLICAN TOGETHER

cans, Congress passed the 15th Amendment, explicitly guaranteeing voting rights for blacks.

The 15th Amendment – the final of the three post-War civil rights Amendments – was the first-ever constitutional expansion of voting rights; and like the two previous civil rights Amendments, it was passed along partisan lines. Not a single one of the 56 Democrats in Congress at that time voted for the 15th Amendment [207] – not one Democrat either from the North or the South supported granting explicit voting rights to black Americans. Yet, despite the opposition from Democrats, the 15th Amendment did pass – passed entirely by Republicans – and its passage was greeted by black Americans with great rejoicing. [208] With the passage of this Amendment, leading abolitionist Wendell Phillips joyfully exclaimed, "We have washed color out of the Constitution!" [209]

GREAT REJOICING OCCURRED AT THE PASSAGE OF THE 15TH AMENDMENT

Just as Republicans had passed several civil rights laws during the Civil War, they passed several more after the war. The first was that of 1866, [210] making it illegal to deprive a person of civil rights because of race, color, or previous servitude. Democrats not only opposed that bill [211] but Democratic President Andrew Johnson even vetoed it; [212] however, Republicans overrode his veto – to the jubilation of both black and white civil rights advocates – and the bill became law. Two other civil rights laws were passed that year, [213] one protecting marriages of blacks and one prohibiting slave-hunting. In 1867, five more civil rights laws

REPUBLICANS PASSED LAWS TO PROTECT MARRIAGE

were passed, providing for voting rights and for the enforcement and protection of other civil rights. [214] Democratic President Andrew Johnson vetoed three of those five bills, [215] but Republicans again overrode his vetoes. Republicans passed two more civil rights laws in

DEMOCRAT PRESIDENT ANDREW JOHNSON
REGULARLY VETOED CIVIL RIGHTS BILLS

REPUBLICAN PRESIDENT ULYSSES S. GRANT
SIGNED CIVIL RIGHTS BILLS

1868, [216] another in 1869, [217] four more in 1870, [218] two more in 1871, [219] one in 1873, [220] and another in 1875. [221] These last nine civil rights bills were passed under Republican President Ulysses S. Grant, who signed rather than vetoed the bills. African Americans watching civil rights progress at the Capitol greeted the passage of civil rights bills with great celebration. [222]

By 1875, only a decade after the Civil War, Republicans had successfully passed almost two-dozen civil rights laws; and black American legislators often played significant roles in the debates surrounding

CELEBRATING THE PASSAGE OF
REPUBLICAN CIVIL RIGHTS BILLS

the passage of these laws. † One such example involved a civil rights bill in 1871 – a bill to allow the federal government to punish Klan violence. During the debates on that bill, Representative Robert Brown Elliott of South Carolina addressed the issue of southern violence and delivered a compelling speech:

REPUBLICAN U.S. REP. ROBERT B. ELLIOTT

> [T]he Democratic Party of the South – as evidenced in the utterances of its recognized organs [official writings] and leaders – . . . exhibits the declared purpose to defeat the ballot with the bullet and other coercive means. . . . I have presented a few of the manifold proofs . . . in support of the facts warranting the passage of this bill. I have shown the declared purpose of the Ku Klux organization, and I refer to the official records of nearly every southern State during the past ten months to show how that bloody purpose has been in part executed. This bill will tend in some degree to prevent its full achievement. I do not wish to be understood as speaking for the colored man alone when I demand instant protection for the loyal men of the South. No sir – my demand is not so restricted. . . . The white Republican of the South is

† To read many of the speeches of these early African American congressional heroes, see the website www.law.nyu.edu/davisp/neglectedvoices/index2.html.

also hunted down and murdered or scourged for his opinion's sake, and during the past two years more than six hundred loyal men of both races have perished in my State alone. Yet, sir, it is true that these masked murderers strike chiefly at the black race.... [S]imply because

he exercises his privileges as an American freeman, you [Democrats] would drive him into exile with the pitiless lash, or doom him to swift murder – seeking your revenge for political power lost by moving at midnight along the path of the assassin! . . . I trust, sir, that this bill will pass quickly, and be quickly enforced, . . . [lest] the Democratic Party triumph in the States of the South through armed violence. [223]

REPUBLICAN U.S. REP. JOSEPH H. RAINEY

Rep. Joseph Hayne Rainey, another member from South Carolina, also delivered a powerful speech during the debates on that bill, explaining why blacks were most often the targets of Klan violence:

When we call to mind the fact that this [Klan] persecution is waged against men for the simple reason that they dare vote with the [Republican] Party that saved the Union intact, . . . [t]he question is sometimes asked, "Why do not the courts of law afford redress?" . . . We answer, that the courts are in many instances under the control of those [Democrats] who are wholly inimical [enemies] to the impartial administration of law and equity. What benefit would result from appeal to tribunals [courts] whose officers are secretly in sympathy with the very evil against which we are striving? . . . If the Negroes – numbering one-eighth of the population of these United States – would only cast their votes in the interest of

AFRICAN AMERICANS CONTINUED TO VOTE
REUBLICAN IN OVERWHELMING NUMBERS

the Democratic Party, all open measures [of violence] against them would be immediately suspended and their rights as American citizens recognized. But . . . I can only say that we love free-

dom more – vastly more – than slavery; consequently we hope to keep clear of the Democrats! . . . I will say that in the State of South Carolina, there is no disturbance of an alarming character in any one of the counties in which the Republicans have a majority. The troubles are usually in those sections in which the Democrats have [control]. . . . I say . . . to the entire membership of the Democratic Party, that upon your hands rests the blood of the loyal men of the South. Disclaim it as you will; the stain is there to prove your criminality before God and the world in the day of retribution which will surely come. I pity the man – or party of men – who would seek to ride into power over the dead body of a legitimate

DEMOCRATS OFTEN TRIUMPHED THROUGH
THE SHEDDING OF INNOCENT BLOOD

opponent. . . . I can say for my people that. . . . we are fully determined to stand by the Republican Party and the government. . . . [W]e have resolved to be loyal and firm, "and [as Queen Esther said long ago], if we perish, we perish!" I earnestly hope the bill will pass. [224]

That bill did pass, but only over the united opposition of Democrats; not one Democrat – either from the North or the South – supported the civil rights bill to punish Klan violence. [225]

Four years later, black Americans again played a significant role in the debates on a civil rights bill – this time the civil rights bill of 1875 to prohibit segregation and racial discrimination. Rep. Richard Cain of South Carolina, a clergyman and bishop of the AME denomination as well as a strong political leader, forcefully rebutted the Democrats' arguments in favor of segregation and discrimination:

I have sat in this House nearly nine months and I have listened to gentlemen recognized as the leaders on the other side [i.e., the Democrats] attempting to demonstrate . . . the inferiority of a race of men whom they have so long outraged, and to cast a slur upon them because they have been helpless. . . . [And t]he [Democratic] gentleman from Virginia calls in question the propriety of passing the

REPUBLICAN U.S. REP. RICHARD CAIN

civil rights bill. I cannot agree with him. . . . Why not pass the civil rights bill? . . . The civil rights bill simply declares this: that there shall be no discriminations between citizens of this land so far as the laws of the land are concerned. I can find no fault with that. The great living principle of the American government is that all men are free. We admit from every land and every nationality men to come here and, under the folds of that noble flag, repose in peace and protection.... Yet because, forsooth [in truth], God Almighty made the face of the Negro black, [Democrats] would deny him that right though he be a man.... Mr. Speaker, I regard the civil rights bill as among the best

measures that ever came before Congress. Why, sir, it is at the very foundation of good government.... I have no fear for the future.... I have faith in this country.... The great principle which underlies our government – of liberty, of justice, of right – will eventually prevail in this land and we shall enjoy equal rights under the laws.... Let the laws of the country be just; let the laws of the country be equitable; this is all we ask, and we will take our chances under the laws in this land.... Place all citizens upon one broad platform; and if the Negro is not qualified to hoe his row in this contest of life, then let him go down. All we ask of this country is to put no barriers between us – to lay no stumbling blocks in our way, to give us freedom to accomplish our destiny.... Do this, sir, and we shall ask nothing more. [226]

Despite these types of powerful speeches, Democrats continued their relentless attacks against the bill. In fact, immediately following one such Democratic tirade against the bill, black Rep. Robert Brown Elliott rose to respond. It was such a climatic moment that artists of the day created illustrations depicting the verbal battle between this black Republican and racist Democrat Alexander Stephens, former Vice President of the Confederacy who was now a leader of the

BLACK REPUBLICAN ROBERT BROWN ELLIOTT DEBATED AND DEFEATED
RACIST DEMOCRAT ALEXANDER STEPHENS

Democrat's arguments against the civil rights bill. [227] Elliott's rebuttal of Stephens was eloquent; he began:

> [I]t is a matter of regret to me that it is necessary at this day that I should rise in the presence of an American Congress to advocate a bill which simply asserts equal rights and equal privileges for all classes of American citizens.... [but] the motive that impels me . . . is as broad as the Constitution. [228]

Elliott explained how black Americans had long fought for American freedom:

> In the events that led to the achievement of American Independence, the Negro . . . bore his part bravely upon many battlefields. . . . [For example, t]he tall granite shaft which a grateful State [Connecticut] has reared above its sons who fell in defending Fort Griswold against the attack of Benedict Arnold [in 1781 at the Battle of Groton Heights] bears the

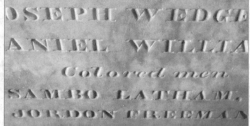

FT. GRISWOLD MONUMENT (LEFT, 134' HIGH) LISTING SOME
OF THE THOUSANDS OF AFRICAN AMERICAN PATRIOTS
(ABOVE) THAT FOUGHT IN THE AMERICAN REVOLUTION

AFRICAN AMERICAN RIFLE MARKSMEN IN THE WAR OF 1812

AFRICAN AMERICAN SOLDIERS IN THE CIVIL WAR

name of Jordan Freeman and other brave men of the African race who there cemented with their blood the cornerstone of the Republic [during the American Revolution]. . . . [And a]t the battle of New Orleans [in the War of 1812], under the immortal Jackson, a colored regiment held the extreme right of the American line unflinchingly and drove back the British column that pressed upon them at the point of the bayonet. . . . [And] in 1861 [during the Civil War]. . . . the Negro – true to that patriotism and love of country that have ever characterized and marked his history on this continent – came to the aid of the government in its efforts to maintain the Constitution. . . . [Now] we are told by the distinguished gentleman from Georgia [Mr. Stephens] † that Congress has no power under the Constitution to pass such a [civil rights] law. . . . [H]as not the judgment of the gentleman from Georgia been warped by the ghost of the dead doctrines of States' Rights? Has he been altogether free from prejudices engendered by long training in that school of politics that well-nigh destroyed this government? . . . I am astonished that

DEMOCRAT ALEXANDER STEPHENS OFTEN LED THE OPPOSITION AGAINST CIVIL RIGHTS BILLS

the gentleman . . . from Georgia should have been so grossly misled. . . . [H]e now offers this government – which he has done his utmost to destroy – a very poor return for its magnanimous [gracious and forgiving] treatment, to come here to seek to continue – by the assertion of doctrines obnoxious to the true principles of our government – the burdens and oppressions which rest upon five millions of his countrymen

† Congressional parliamentary procedure requires that in any debate, the individual speaking may not directly address any person except the chairman, and that he may not at any time address any other member of the body by name. Therefore, speakers (as Elliott did here) used terms such as "the distinguished gentleman" or "the gentleman from Georgia" rather than "you" or "Mr. Stephens."

– [slaves] who never failed to lift their earnest prayers for the success of this government when the gentleman [Mr. Stephens] was asking to break up the Union of these States and to blot the American Republic from the galaxy of nations. Sir, it is scarcely twelve years since that gentleman shocked the civilized world by announcing the birth of a government which rested on human slavery as its cornerstone. † The progress of events has swept away that pseudo-government which rested on greed, pride, and tyranny; and the race whom he then ruthlessly spurned and trampled on are here to meet him in debate and to demand that the rights which are enjoyed by their former op-pressors who vainly sought to overthrow a government which they could not prostitute to the base uses of slavery. . . . The gentleman from Georgia has learned much since 1861, but he is still a laggard [behind the times]. . . . Let him lend his influence . . . to complete the proud structure of legislation which makes this nation worthy of the great Declaration [of Independence] which heralded its birth, and he will have done that which will most nearly redeem his reputation. [229]

Elliott's magnificent response did not convert Alexander Stephens or the other Democrats, but it was so eloquent that it silenced them. In fact, the Democrats' rebuttal against Elliott was so weak that the best they could do was to claim that the speech was not really his – that it was so brilliant that someone else must have written it – that surely a black American such as Elliott could not have created such a masterful speech. [230] That Democratic response against Elliott's eloquence is reminiscent of an old lawyers' adage that admonishes: "When you have the facts on your side, argue the facts. When you have the law on your side, argue the law. When neither is on your side, change the subject and question the mo-tives of the opposition." That was exactly the approach taken by the Democrats against Elliott. He so completely befuddled them

---

† See the picture and note about the origins of this phrase on pp. 27-28.

with his oratorical skills that all they could do was claim someone else must have written his speech.

REPUBLICAN U.S. REP.
JOHN R. LYNCH

Rep. John Roy Lynch of Mississippi, in closing his speech on the same bill, predicted what he believed would be the outcome of the vote:

> In conclusion, Mr. Speaker, I say to the Republican Members of the House that the passage of this bill is expected by you. If any of our Democratic friends will vote for it, we will be agreeably surprised. But if Republicans should vote against it, we will be sorely disappointed. . . . But I have no fears whatever in this respect. You [Republicans] have stood by the colored people of this country when it was more unpopular to do so than it is to pass this bill. You have fulfilled every promise thus far, and I have no reason to believe that you will not fulfill this one. [231]

That civil rights bill did pass, but regrettably, Rep. Lynch did not receive the surprise he had hoped for; it was exactly as he had suspected: not a single one of the 114 Democrats in Congress voted for that civil rights bill; [232] that bill – like the other civil rights bills – was passed by the Republicans over strident and virtually unanimous opposition of Democrats. However, this is not surprising considering the Democrats' attitude at that time. As explained by Democratic presidential candidate Horace Greeley:

DEMOCRAT HORACE GREELEY

> The Democratic Party of today is simply the Rebellion [the Confederacy] seeking to achieve its essential purposes within and through the Union. A victory which does

not enable it [the Democratic Party] to put its feet on the necks of the black race seems to the bulk of its adherents not worth having. . . . It clings to that exaggerated notion of States' rights which makes them the shield of all manner of wrongs and abuses. [233]

That 1875 civil rights bill was the last of the almost two-dozen civil rights bills passed under Republicans. In fact, following the passage of that 1875 bill, it would be another 89 years before the next civil rights law was passed. Why did the remarkable progress come to an abrupt halt after 1875? Because in 1876 Democrats gained control of the U. S. House for the first time since 1865; therefore, with a divided Congress, Democrats successfully blocked any further progress in the civil rights arena. Facing such strident and irrational Democratic obstructionists, the enthusiasm for fighting in that arena soon waned and civil rights momentum was lost.

However, not only did Democrats gain the U. S. House in 1876 but also they were able to bring Reconstruction to a close by having all federal troops withdrawn from the South, thus removing the final protective barrier between black Americans and those Democrats aggressively seeking to violate their new-found civil rights. That federal protection had been crucial to black Americans at that time, for as a Republican election official from Mississippi explained in 1868:

The Rebels never needed protection; they have had it all the time; it is only the Republicans – the Negroes especially – . . . who need protection. [234]

The reason for the 1876 withdrawal of federal troops from the South had been the results of the presidential election between Republican Rutherford B. Hayes and Democrat Samuel Tilden. A total of 185 electoral votes had been needed to win the presidency and when the votes were counted, Democrat Tilden had received 184 electoral votes and Republican Hayes had received 165. Although neither had received the necessary votes to win, there was a total of 20 disputed electoral

1876 PRESIDENTIAL CANDIDATES, SAMUEL TILDEN (D-LEFT) AND RUTHERFORD B. HAYES (R-RIGHT)

votes that had not yet been counted. [235] If Republican Hayes received all 20 of those votes, he would became President; if Democrat Tilden received even one of those votes, then he would became President.

The uncounted votes came primarily from the three disputed southern States of Florida, Louisiana, and South Carolina. In those three States, dual election results had been reported. One tally in Florida showed Republicans had won; the other tally showed Democrats had won; the same was true in South Carolina and Louisiana. Why were there disputed results – why two different tallies of votes? Because in each of those three States, Democrats had been extremely active both in suppressing the black vote through violence and in altering the counts at the ballot box. One newspaper illustration depicted the type of violence that helped alter the count: a Democrat is inviting blacks to come vote, but notice that inside, an armed gunman sits waiting beside the ballot box to ensure that the black voter reaches the "right" decision (see illustration on the next page). [236] Consequently, many blacks did not even try to vote. [237]

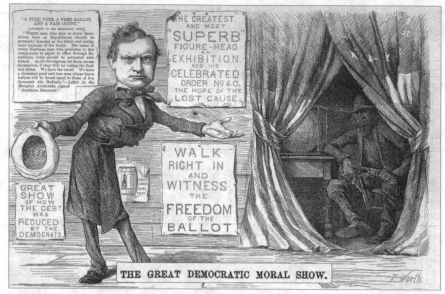

THE GREAT DEMOCRATIC MORAL SHOW.

(African American U. S. Rep. John Roy Lynch later personally experienced the same type of vote-counting difficulties as had Rutherford B. Hayes. Lynch explained that these difficulties had come from those Democrats whom he described as "the ballot box stuffer [and] the shotgun holder of the South." [238] He therefore declared:

> I say to you, gentlemen, that in my State, the "official return" is an official fraud. When I ran for Congress in the Sixth District of Mississippi in 1880, I know that there were not less than 5,000 votes for me that were counted for the [Democrat] that ran against me. Now bear in mind, the official report gave him 5,000 of my votes. [If these fraudulent votes for him are counted, then] you say to me: "We will only admit you on what the Democrats choose to give you." Now, I say that is wrong. [239])

Voter fraud by Democrats was indeed a problem in the South. In addition to changing the voting counts or intimidating voters, *Harper's Weekly* showed another way that southern Democrats were able to obtain additional votes: they simply took the names off cemetery headstones and then cast a fraudulent vote in the name of a dead voter. [240]

Returning to the 1876 presidential election, it was discovered not only that the Democrats had engaged in widespread voter fraud and intimidation at the local level but that Democratic presidential candidate Samuel Tilden's campaign had actually engaged in direct bribery of election officials in the disputed States. [241] Therefore, by keeping black Americans from voting in the disputed States and by corruptly altering the voting counts, Democrats claimed that they had won those

HOW THE COPPERHEADS OBTAIN THEIR VOTES.

DEMOCRATS REGISTERING NEW VOTERS

three States. However, the Republicans counted the suppressed African American votes and ignored the fraudulent votes, asserting that they had won those three States.

Since the Electoral College did not count any of the disputed votes, and since neither presidential candidate could win the election without them, the U. S. House was required to decide who would become President. [†] Congress therefore convened a commission of 15 members to hear the issue, a commission composed of 5 members

† It is the 12th Amendment of the Constitution that requires that the U. S. House must choose the President in any election in which one candidate does not receive a majority of the Electoral College vote. The 12th Amendment specifically stipulates: "the person having the greatest number of votes for President shall be the President if such number be a majority of the whole number of electors appointed; and if no person have such majority, then from the persons having the highest numbers not exceeding three on the list of those voted for as President, the House of Representatives shall choose immediately by ballot the President."

from the House, 5 from the Senate, and 5 from the Supreme Court. Since the House was in Democratic control, 3 of its 5 members were Democrats; since the Senate was in Republican control, 3 of its 5 members were Republicans. From the Supreme Court, 2 of its 5 members were Republicans, 2 were Demo-

THE 1876 PRESIDENTIAL ELECTION COMMISSION

crats, and 1 was an Independent. Thus, the commission was made up of 7 Democrats, 7 Republicans, and 1 Independent. However, the 1 Independent resigned from the Supreme Court and went home to become a State Senator. Since the only remaining members of the Supreme Court were Republicans, the departed member was replaced with a Republican, meaning that the Commission was composed of 7 Democrats and 8 Republicans. [242]

The Commission investigated and determined that there had been voter suppression through the killing, injuring, and intimidation of black Americans by Democrats; the Commission therefore – by an 8-7 vote – awarded the election to Republican Rutherford B. Hayes. [243] The Democratic House, however, refused to ratify the findings of the Commission and a filibuster was threatened. [244] The result was that America had no President.

ANNOUNCING THE COMMISSION REPORT

DEMOCRATS REFUSE TO RATIFY THE RESULTS

The election controversy continued for four months until a solution was proposed – a solution now called "The Great Compromise." The Democrats offered to ratify the Commission's report – but only if the last federal troops were withdrawn from Florida, Louisiana, and South Carolina. If Republicans did not agree, and if federal troops were not removed from those three States, America would remain without a President. The proposal was finally agreed to. [245] Federal troops therefore were withdrawn from the three remaining States in which they had been stationed, thus officially ending Reconstruction in the South; [246] Rutherford B. Hayes became President.

RUTHERFORD B. HAYES BECAME PRESIDENT

Following the withdrawal of the last federal troops, the South became known as the "solid Democratic South." [247] Southern State legislatures were again solidly in the hands of Democrats, and white supremacy in the South was reestablished. [248]

It was during this same contested election in Florida that the Democrats for a second time challenged the credentials of African American Rep. Josiah Walls, and the Democratically controlled House sent him home. Walls had survived the first challenge when Republicans were in charge of the House, but after being sent home by the Democrats (and with Florida back in the hands of Democrats as a result of "The Great Compromise"), Walls was defeated by white Democrats in the next election, thus ending his congressional career. [249] Eventually, all remaining black legislators

REPUBLICAN U.S. REP. JOSIAH WALLS

in the other southern Democratic States were defeated and removed from Congress. Democrats therefore succeeded in barring southern blacks from federal elected offices for an additional 70 years. [250]

Returning to 1876, since control of the federal Congress at that time was split between Republicans and Democrats, and since no more civil rights laws were being passed, public debate began to focus on issues that had already been raised in earlier civil rights laws that Democrats were now trying to reverse – such as educational policy. For example, a piece entitled *Politics and the School Question: Attitude of the Republican and Democratic Parties in 1876*, [251] examined the contrasting positions of the two parties on the issue of education. The Republicans had supported public education for all children, regardless of race; [252] Democrats not only opposed such public education but in fact strongly supported segregated education.

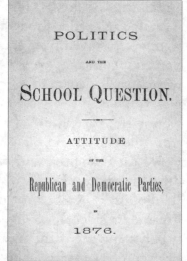

REPUBLICANS SUPPORTED PUBLIC EDUCATION FOR AFRICAN AMERICANS, WHILE DEMOCRATS SUPPORTED NO EDUCATION, OR SEGREGATED EDUCATION, FOR AFRICAN AMERICANS

As an example, Democratic Congressman James Harper of North Carolina published and widely distributed a pro-segregation speech entitled: "Separate Schools for White and Colored with Equal Advantages; Mixed Schools Never!" [253] Similarly, in 1875, the Democratic Executive Committee of Ohio issued a piece on public education to "expose" what they called the "tricks" of the Republican Executive Committee. [254] And what were the so-called dirty "tricks" of Republicans to which Democrats objected?

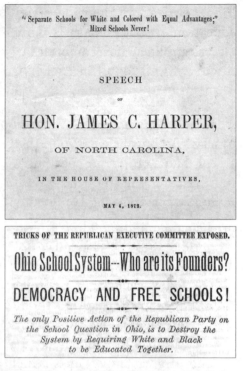

In what was intended to be an insult, Democrats complained, "The only Positive Action of the Republican Party on the School Question in Ohio, is to Destroy the System by Requiring White and Black to be Educated Together." [255]

The Democrats' response against open education for black youth sometimes went beyond words to acts of violence – as when they burned down eight schools in Memphis in which black youth were being taught. [256] Additionally, since churches in the South frequently provided education for youth (such as St. Philips in Richmond; [257] see below, right), churches were also frequently burned down. [258]

DEMOCRATS OFTEN BURNED DOWN SCHOOLS AND CHURCHES THAT TAUGHT AFRICAN AMERICANS

The evidence of the widespread Democratic opposition to equal education for black youth is numerous and abundant – and black Americans knew how important a good education was to their own future. As Rep. John Roy Lynch had accurately noted:

[N]o educated people can be held in bondage. [259]

Black leaders understood that good education was vital not only to black Americans but also to the future of the entire country. Rep. Joseph Hayne Rainey – speaking on a bill to strengthen the education system for all students, including young black students – wisely reminded the opposing Democrats:

> I shall remind the House of one thing more. . . . The youth now springing up to manhood will be the future lawmakers and rulers of our country. That they should be intelligent and thoroughly educated is a prime necessity and of great importance, which is admitted by all and denied by none. All that may be done with this end in view will be returned with an increased interest. I truly hope that those [Democrats] who oppose this bill will reconsider their opposition and give it their vote when the question shall again be before the House. For one, I shall give it my hearty support, believing it to be just and beneficial in its provisions. [260]

REPUBLICAN U.S. REP. JOSEPH H. RAINEY

Unfortunately, 87 percent of the Democrats in Congress at that time voted against that education bill. [261] Segregated, inferior, and dilapidated schools for blacks became the norm in the southern States under Democratic control. [262]

In 1954, the Supreme Court in *Brown* v. *Board of Education* [263] finally struck down State segregation laws in education, thus reinstating what Republicans had done nearly seventy-five years earlier in the 1875 civil rights bill. What was the southern Democratic response to the Court decision finally ending segregated education? There was a two-fold response: one of words, and one of actions.

In the category of words, 100 Democrats in the U. S. Congress – 19 Senators and 81 Representatives – passed the "Southern Manifesto" denouncing the Court's decision to end segregation. [264] Those 100 Democrats declared (in 1956!) that desegregation was "certain to destroy the system of public education" and that there would be what they called an "explosive and dangerous condition created by this decision." [265] Also in the category of words, Democratic Governor Herman Talmadge of Georgia issued a written attack on the Court decision and promised that there "will never be mixed schools while I am Governor"; he even warned of forthcoming "bloodshed" because of the desegregation decision. [266] Mississippi Democratic Governor James Coleman, when asked in an interview on "Meet the Press" whether the public schools of Mississippi would ever be integrated, succinctly replied, "I would say that a baby born in Mississippi today will never live long enough to see an integrated school." [267] This was typical of what many southern Democrats did in the category of words.

But the Democratic response went beyond words and also included actions. Following the 1954 school desegregation decision, southern Democratic Governors went to extreme lengths to keep the Court decision from going into effect. For example, in 1956, Democratic Governor Allan Shivers of Texas deployed the Texas Rangers to keep blacks from entering public schools in Mansfield. [268] The following year, 1957, Democratic Governor Orval Faubus of Arkansas called out the National Guard to keep black students from entering Central

DEMOCRAT GOV. ALLAN SHIVERS

High School in Little Rock. [269] However, Republican President Dwight D. Eisenhower quickly intervened and federalized the Arkansas National Guard to take it away from Governor Faubus. Eisenhower then replaced the Arkansas Guard with 1,200 troops from the elite 101st Air-

ARKANSAS DEMOCRAT GOVERNOR ORVAL FAUBUS (LEFT) FOUGHT FOR SEGREGATION;
REPUBLICAN PRESIDENT DWIGHT D. EISENHOWER (RIGHT) FOUGHT FOR INTEGRATION

borne Division, ordering them to protect the nine black students who had chosen to go to Central High. [270] Democrats in the U. S. Senate strongly protested Eisenhower's actions to protect these black students. For example, Georgia Democratic Senator Richard Russell specifically complained about using "the whole might of the federal government, including the armed forces . . . , to force a commingling of white and Negro children in the State-supported schools of the State." [271] (Apparently, in the minds of many southern Democrats, the State-supported schools of a State were not to be open to black students in the State.)

Georgia Democratic Governor Marvin Griffin also attacked Eisenhower's actions, and praised Arkansas Governor Faubus for his attempt to prevent blacks from entering Central High School. Governor Griffin promised that as long as he held office, he would "maintain segregation in the schools; and the races will not be mixed, come hell or high water." [272] To prepare for the possibility that Eisenhower might do in Georgia what he had done in Arkansas, legislation was introduced in the Democrat-controlled Georgia legislature so that if desegregation were attempted, the public schools of the State would be dissolved and replaced with State-run private schools so that blacks could be excluded. [273] These types of schools became known as "segregation academies." [274]

Meanwhile in Arkansas, Democratic Governor Faubus, unable to prevent black students from attending school because of the federal protection they received, simply shut down the schools for the next year to prevent further attendance. [275] And Virginia Democratic Governor James Almond – like other southern Democratic Governors – shut down public schools rather than permit black students to attend. [276]

In 1960 in Louisiana, where Democratic Governor Jimmie Davis supported segregation, [277] four federal marshals were required to accompany little Ruby Bridges so that she could attend a public elementary school in New Orleans. When Ruby entered that class, every other parent withdrew their children and for the entire year, little Ruby was the only student in that classroom – just Ruby and her schoolteacher from Boston. [278]

So deep-seated was the racism among southern Democratic leaders that when the 1964 civil rights bill became law, Lester Maddox, who became Democratic Governor of Georgia, sold the fast-food business he owned rather than serve blacks in his restaurant. [279] And in 1960,

DEMOCRAT GOVERNOR GEORGE TIMMERMAN (LEFT) CLOSED STATE FACILITIES TO EVANGELIST BILLY GRAHAM (RIGHT) BECAUSE GRAHAM INCLUDED AFRICAN AMERICANS IN HIS RALLIES

Mississippi Democratic Governor Hugh White had even requested that evangelist Billy Graham segregate his crusades [280] – something Graham refused to do. And when South Carolina Democratic Governor George Timmerman learned that Billy Graham had invited African Americans to a Reformation Rally at the State Capitol, he promptly denied use of the facilities to the evangelist. [281]

This type of Democratic response against black Americans – and against the whites who supported them – was common across much of the South; and the reasons given by Democratic leaders to justify this disgusting behavior was simply, "States' Rights" [282] – the same rhetoric they had used a century earlier, first to justify slavery and the creation of a slave-holding nation and then to enact laws enforcing segregation and withholding voting rights from black Americans for the next eighty years after the Civil War. [283] During the era of desegregation,

in an effort to remake the image of racism so long and so properly associated with the southern cry of "States Rights," southern leaders began to claim that the southern Confederate battle flag – the quintessential symbol of a perverted States' Rights philosophy – was actually a symbol of heritage rather than hate. [284] Consequently,

THE CONFEDERATE FLAG *IS* ABOUT HERITAGE, BUT IT IS THE WRONG KIND OF HERITAGE

many today wrongly – but innocently – believe that the battle flag of the South is about heritage and not about hate – something easily refuted by historical facts and documents.

Returning to the school desegregation situation, some southern Democratic Governors did work for integration – including Tennessee Governor Frank Clement, Florida Governor LeRoy Collins, and

DEMOCRAT GOVERNORS CLEMENT (LEFT) AND CHANDLER (RIGHT) WORKED FOR INTEGRATION

Kentucky Governor Happy Chandler – but these tended to be the exceptions among southern Democratic Governors rather than the rule, and their admirable behavior was clearly overshadowed by the negative behavior of the others.

Democratic leaders long stood in the doorways of schoolhouses and told black school children that we don't want you in here to get the good education that our children are getting. Today, as many black students have become mired in urban schools that are often failing or deteriorating, Democrats are once again standing in the doorway, this time to keep black students from getting out.

Consider the situation in Washington, D. C., where 84 percent of the city's students are black: [285] despite the fact that nearly $13,500 is spent each year on every student in the District [286] (an amount almost twice the national average of $7,500 per student [287]), D. C. schools currently rank among the worst of all schools in the nation. [288] Congress therefore moved to help by providing a $7,500 voucher for low-income students trapped in failing schools – a voucher they could redeem to attend a better school – a school chosen by that student and his or her parents. When that congressional proposal came to a vote, ninety-nine percent of Democrats voted *against* that bill allowing students in failing schools to choose a better school – only one percent of Democrats in Congress supported vouchers and parental school choice in education, [289] even though nationally nearly 70 percent of African Americans with children support educational choice [290] – a level of support well above that of the general population. [291]

While Democrats once stood in the doorways of public schools and told black students, "We don't want you in here," they are again standing in the doorways of public schools, this time telling black students that they don't want them out – that they want them to remain in failing schools. It appears that for a century-and-a-half, Democrats have often taken wrong positions on educational opportunity for black Americans.

Returning to the 19th century, in 1883, the U. S. Supreme Court – using the same abominable logic it displayed in the deplorable *Dred Scott*

THE SUPREME COURT PROLONGED SEGREGATION FOR A
CENTURY BY STRIKING DOWN EARLY CIVIL RIGHTS LAWS

decision – struck down the 1875 civil rights laws that prohibited segregation and racial discrimination. [292] Regrettably, it would be almost seventy years after this before the Supreme Court would relent [293] and partially undo some of the painful effects of its pro-segregation decision by reinstating part of the intent of the Republican civil rights law of 1875.

Rep. John Roy Lynch, a Congressman from Mississippi mentioned earlier, had grown up as a slave until freed by the Emancipation Proclamation in 1863. Within a decade, he had become Speaker of the House in Mississippi and later received presidential appointments from Republican Presidents Benjamin Harrison and William McKinley. Lynch

REPUBLICAN U.S. REP. JOHN R. LYNCH

was appointed an army officer during the Spanish-American War, earned a law degree, and was the Chairman of the Republican Party in Mississippi. [294] He was a leader who served his State and nation well. Despite the serious racial problems of his day, Lynch's love for his country was still very evident and reflected the patriotism still present among African Americans today:

I love the land that gave me birth; I love the Stars and Stripes. This country is where I intend to live – where I expect to die. To preserve the honor of the national flag and to maintain perpetually the Union of the States, hundreds – and I may say thousands – of noble, brave, and true-hearted colored men have fought, bled, and died. [295]

In 1884, John Roy Lynch became the first black American to pre-side over a national political convention – the Republican National

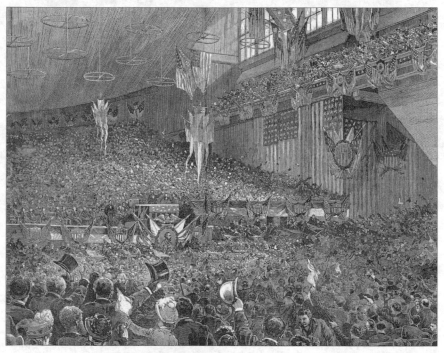

REP. JOHN R. LYNCH WAS THE FIRST AFRICAN AMERICAN TO PRESIDE OVER A NATIONAL
POLITICAL CONVENTION – THE 1884 REPUBLICAN NATIONAL CONVENTION IN CHICAGO

Convention in Chicago. [296] While Lynch was the first black Ameri-can to preside over a national political convention, he was not the last: U. S. Senator Edward Brooke presided over the 1968 Republican National Convention, [297] and Rep. J. C. Watts presided over the 2000 Republican National Convention. [298] While three black Americans have presided over National Conventions for Republicans, to date Democrats have never had a black American preside over any of their National Democratic Conventions. (Yvonne Brathwaite Burke did serve as a Vice-Chair of the Democratic Convention of 1972, [299] but not its chair or even its co-chair.)

Following the removal of federal troops from the South after the agree-ment of 1876, federal troops could no longer protect African American voting. Republicans therefore sought different means to preserve the rights of black Americans in the South. For example, they posted hand-bills reminding southern Democrats first of the federal laws protecting black voting rights and then warning of huge fines for violations. [300]

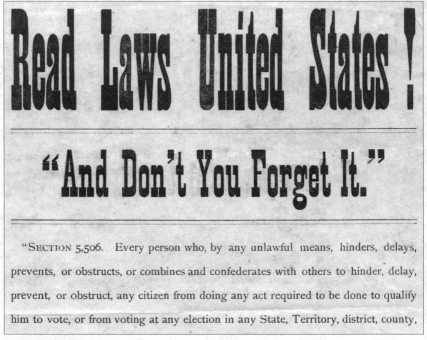

Read Laws United States !

"And Don't You Forget It."

"SECTION 5,506. Every person who, by any unlawful means, hinders, delays, prevents, or obstructs, or combines and confederates with others to hinder, delay, prevent, or obstruct, any citizen from doing any act required to be done to qualify him to vote, or from voting at any election in any State, Territory, district, county,

A POSTER TO REMIND DEMOCRATS OF FEDERAL LAWS PROTECTING AFRICAN AMERICAN VOTING

The presidential election of that year (1880) was between Republican James A. Garfield (a minister of the Gospel, a Union General, and a war hero) and Northern Democrat Winfield Scott

Hancock. Hancock had been a successful Union General during the Civil War, but after the War he was reassigned because of his leniency toward unreconstructed Democrats. [301] (Recall that northern, or

GEN. GARFIELD   GEN. HANCOCK

Union Democrats such as Hancock, sought to preserve the Union but not to end slavery or grant equality to African Americans.) Because Hancock was a Democrat (even though he had fought for the Union), a handbill was issued to remind citizens why they should _not_ vote Democratic in that election.

The reasons given in that piece would today be considered as inflammatory language; at that time, however, the declarations were nothing more than reminders – that is, the facts recorded in that piece were already widely known by the voters of that day:

Why I Will not Vote the Democratic Ticket.

I am opposed to the Democratic Party, and I will tell you why.

Every State that seceded from the United States was a Democratic State. . . .

Every man that shot Union soldiers was a Democrat. . . .

Every man that loved slavery better than liberty was a Democrat.

The man that assassinated Abraham Lincoln was a Democrat.

Every man that sympathized with the assassin – every man glad that the noblest President ever elected was assassinated – was a Democrat. . . .

Every man that wept over the corpse of slavery was a Democrat.

Every man that cursed Lincoln because he issued the Proclamation of Emancipation – the grandest paper since the Declaration of Independence – every one of them was a Democrat. . . .

Soldiers! Every scar you have got on your heroic bodies was given you by a Democrat. Every scar, every arm that is lacking, every limb that is gone, every scar is a souvenir of a Democrat.

That handbill then contrasted the Republicans with the Democrats:

Why I Will not Vote the Democratic Ticket.

I am opposed to the Democratic Party, and I will tell you why. Every State that seceded from the United States was a Democratic State. Every ordinance of secession that was drawn was drawn by a Democrat. Every man that endeavored to tear the old flag from the heaven that it enriches was a Democrat. Every enemy this great Republic has had for twenty years has been a Democrat. Every man that shot Union soldiers was a Democrat. Every man that starved Union soldiers and refused them in the extremity of death a crust was a Democrat. Every man that tried to destroy this nation was a Democrat. Every man that loved slavery better than liberty was a Democrat. The man that assassinated Abraham Lincoln was a Democrat. Every man that sympathized with the assassin—every man glad that the noblest President ever elected was assassinated—was a Democrat. Every man that impaired the credit of the United States; every man that swore we would never pay the bonds; every man that swore we would never redeem the greenbacks was a Democrat. Every man that resisted the draft was a Democrat. Every man that wept over the corpse of slavery was a Democrat. Every man that cursed Lincoln because he issued the Proclamation of Emancipation—the grandest paper since the Declaration of Independence—every one of them was a Democrat. Every man that wanted an uprising in the North, that wanted to release the rebel prisoners, that they might burn down the homes of Union soldiers above the heads of their wives and children, while the brave husbands, the heroic fathers, were in the front fighting for the honor of the old flag, every one of them was a Democrat. Every man that believed this glorious nation of ours is only a confederacy, every man that believed the old banner carried by our fathers through the Revolution, through the war of 1812, carried by our brothers over the plains of Mexico, carried by our brothers over the fields of the Rebellion, simply stood for a contract, simply stood for an agreement, was a Democrat. Every man who believed that any State could go out of the Union at its pleasure; every man that believed the grand fabric of the American Government could be made to crumble instantly into dust at the touch of treason was a Democrat.

Soldiers! Every scar you have got on your heroic bodies was given you by a Democrat. Every scar, every arm that is lacking, every limb that is gone, every scar is a souvenir of a Democrat.

WHAT THE REPUBLICAN PARTY HAS NOT DONE.

The Republicans have done some noble things—things that will be remembered as long as there is history. But there are some things they did not do.

They did not use an army to force slavery into Kansas.
They did not fire upon Fort Sumter.
They did not attempt secession.
They did not plunder the nation of its arms.
They did not inaugurate rebellion.
They did not drive American commerce from the seas.
They did not "huzza" over Union disasters.
They did not "huzza" over Rebel victories.
They did not mourn over Rebel defeats.
They did not oppose enlistments in the Union army.
They were not draft rioters.
They were not "Knights of the Golden Circle."
They did not commit the attrocities of Libby, Belle Isle, Salisbury and Andersonville.
They did not oppose emancipation.
They were not "Ku-Klux."
They did not commit the Butchery at Fort Pillow.
They did not commit the horrible massacre at New Orleans.
They did not murder Dixon.
They did not butcher the Chisholm family.
They did not massacre black men at Hamburg.
They did not scourge, and hang, and shoot, and murder men for opinion's sake.
They did not organize the Louisiana white league or the South Carolina rifle clubs.
They did not drench the South with the blood of inoffensive colored men.
They did not invent the "Mississippi plan."
They did not use tissue ballots.
They are not "moonshiners."
They do not resist the national authority.
They did not set up their States above the nation.
They did not try to destroy the Nation's credit.
They do not try to pauperize the American mechanic.
They have not been an impediment to national growth.
They have not been a hindrance to the peoples' prosperity.
Can the Democratic party and all Democrats say as much? The people can trust a party that has not done these things, but they cannot trust a party that in whole or in part did do them.

1880 VOTER HANDBILL

The Republicans have done some noble things – things that will be remembered as long as there is history. But there are some things they did not do.

They did not use an army to force slavery into Kansas. . . .

They were not "Knights of the Golden Circle." † . . . .

They did not oppose emancipation.

They were not "Ku-Klux" . . .

They did not scourge, and hang, and shoot, and murder men for opinion's sake.

They did not organize the Louisiana white league or the South Carolina rifle clubs.

They did not drench the South with the blood of inoffensive colored men. . . .

The piece concluded with a simple question:

Can the Democratic Party and all Democrats say as much? [302]

BANNERS BY WHICH DEMOCRATS WERE KNOWN

A further indication that the Democrats were well known for their bloody atrocities against blacks is seen in an illustration from *Harpers' Weekly* showing the major elements and influences of the Democratic Party. [303] The illustration showed the various banners under which Democrats gathered, and those banners included the Stars and Bars carried by Confederate soldiers; the pro-slavery banner; the Ku Klux Klan banner; the New York Rioters banner (referring to the massive riots instigated against blacks by the Democrats

† See the information about this group on p. 24.

in New York, leading to the killing and injuring of as many as one thousand citizens [304]); and finally the Democrats' banner of repudiation (referring to the Democrats' opposition to paying the national debt incurred in putting down the southern pro-slavery rebellion). [305] These were the various movements led by Democrats, and Americans in that day knew exactly what Democrats stood for.

By the 1880s, a movement called "Southern Redemption" had begun in earnest. Southern Redemption was a political movement to "redeem" the south from the Reconstruction Acts and civil rights laws passed by Republicans – laws and acts that southern Democrats believed threatened their version of a southern society. [306] So firmly were southern Democrats opposed to the constitutional amendments and civil rights laws imposed on them during Reconstruction that one southern newspaper (the *Louisville Courier-Journal*) declared:

> It is safe to say that had the southern people known in 1865 what was in store for them, they would not have laid down their arms – and should not have laid them down. [307]

Southern Redemption was the effort of southern Democrats to restore the South to the racial condition of white supremacy that had existed before the Civil War. The best way for the newly restored Democratic legislatures to "redeem" their State from what had occurred to them following the Civil War was to deprive black Americans of their political rights by the passage of State laws that restricted, removed, or even blatantly violated their civil rights [308] as well as through the prompt repeal of State reconstruction laws that had suppressed Klan violence. [309] Rep. John Roy Lynch – who not only had helped pass the original federal civil rights laws but had also witnessed their subsequent violation at the State level throughout the

DEMOCRATS CONGRATULATING THEMSELVES
ON THEIR VICTORY OVER AFRICAN AMERICANS

period of Southern Redemption – accurately noted:

> The opposition to civil rights in the South . . . is confined
> almost exclusively to States under Democratic control. [310]

Democrats understood how important it was to their survival to
prevent blacks from voting. In fact, an illustration from that period
showed an allegory of the Bible story of Samson, [311] who lost his strength
when his hair was cut. [312] In that illustration, the woman – named
"Southern Democracy" – has used her razor – called "the lost cause

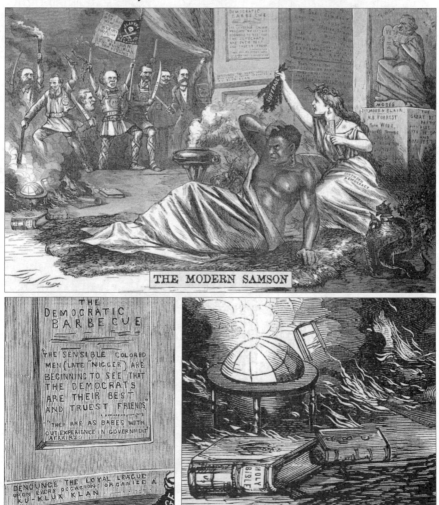

THE MODERN SAMSON

SOUTHERN DEMOCRATS REMOVED VOTING RIGHTS FROM AFRICAN AMERICANS

DEMOCRATIC GROUPS REJOICING OVER THE LOSS OF VOTING RIGHTS FOR AFRICAN AMERICANS

regained" – to cut the black Samson's hair and cause him to lose his strength; and what is his hair – his strength? It is called "suffrage," or voting. With the strength – or the vote – of black Americans removed, various Democratic groups and leaders were rejoicing in the background: Confederates, the KKK, pro-slavery forces, and several famous Democratic leaders of that day, including General Nathan Bedford Forrest, the first Grand Wizard of the Klan (see illustrations on previous page). By the way, notice the phrase "The Democratic Barbecue" and that Democrats are burning various books in the foreground, including the Holy Bible (see close insets on previous page.) As this illustration confirmed, limiting black voting became the major goal for southern Democrats.

Given the explicit federal voting protections that had been established by the 14th and 15th Amendments and the numerous federal civil rights laws, it was no easy task for Democrats to circumvent those protections. It required devious and cunning methods, and southern Democratic legislatures implemented almost a dozen separate devices to deprive blacks of political representation and to keep them from voting.

The first device was the poll tax, a fee paid by a voter before he could vote. The fee was high enough that most poor were unable to pay the tax and therefore were unable to vote; and while some southern whites were poor, nearly all southern blacks were poor, having just emerged from slavery and not yet having established an independent means of living. Democrats in Tennessee enacted a poll tax in 1870, as did Democrats in Delaware in 1873 (after announcing that they were not morally bound by any of the three post-war civil rights amendments to the Constitution). [313] In 1874, Texas proposed a poll tax right after Democrats reclaimed power from Republicans; [314] in 1876, North Carolina enacted a poll tax; [315] and other Democratic States followed. [316]

Literacy tests were the second means that Democrats used to disenfranchise blacks. Literacy tests required a voter to demonstrate a certain level of specific knowledge before he could vote. In some cases, the test was 20 pages long for blacks, and those administering the tests were white Democrats who nearly always ruled that blacks were illiterate. [317] Don't misunderstand: literacy tests were not about whether someone could read or write; these literacy tests often contained questions requiring a

DEMOCRATS USED DISCRIMINATORY LITERACY TESTS
TO PREVENT AFRICAN AMERICANS FROM VOTING

knowledge of obscure and little-known facts. For example, in Alabama the test included questions such as, "Where do presidential electors cast ballots for president?" or "Name the rights a person has after he has been indicted by a grand jury." [318] Ironically, Democrats steadfastly opposed sound education for blacks but then required that blacks have an above average education before they could vote! Clearly, these southern Democrats did not intend for blacks to vote.

The third device used to disenfranchise black Americans was "Grandfather" clauses. "Grandfather" clauses were laws passed by Democratic legislatures allowing only those individuals to vote whose father or grandfather had been registered to vote prior to the passage of the 15th Amendment. [319] Since voting in the South for decades prior to that Amendment had been almost exclusively by whites, this law ensured that poor and illiterate whites could vote but not blacks.

The fourth device was suppressive election procedures. This included the use of "multiple ballots." That is, a Republican voter might be required to cast a ballot in up to eight separate locations – or sometimes to vote for each individual Republican on the ballot at a separate location – before the ballot would be counted. Democratic officials often failed to inform black voters of this complicated procedure and their ballots were therefore disqualified. [320] Democrats also used what were called "hide-and-seek polling places," moving voting boxes to unknown locations at the last minute and then posting armed guards in case any black should stumble upon the hidden voting box. [321]

The fifth device included the use of so-called Black Codes (later called Jim Crow laws) to restrict the freedoms and economic opportunities of blacks. Rep. Robert Brown Elliott reported:

REPUBLICAN U.S. REP.
ROBERT BROWN ELLIOTT

Among the first acts of legislation adopted by several of the [southern Democratic] States . . . were laws which imposed upon the colored race onerous [oppressive] disabilities and burdens and curtailed their rights in the pursuit of life, liberty, and property to such an extent that their freedom was of little value. . . . They [colored citizens] were, in some States, forbidden to appear in the towns. . . . They were required to reside on and cultivate the soil – without the right to purchase or own it. They were excluded from any occupations of gain [i.e., paying jobs] and were not permitted to give testimony in the courts in any case where a white man was a party. [322]

Beginning as early as 1865, southern Democrats passed Black Codes to prevent blacks from holding office, owning agricultural property, entering towns without permission, serving on juries, racially intermarrying, or voting. [323] They even passed – in flagrant violation of the U. S. Constitution – laws preventing blacks from owning knifes or firearms, thus exposing them to Klan violence without any way to defend themselves. [324] National observers at that time concluded that the Democratic South was simply trying to institute a new form of slavery through the use of these Black Codes. [325] Representative Richard Cain of South Carolina agreed:

DEMOCRATIC LAWS LEFT BLACKS
UNPROTECTED AGAINST THE KLAN

When the government of the United States had made the
black man free – when Congress, in the greatness of its magna-
nimity [generosity] prepared to give to every class of men their
rights, and in reconstructing the southern States guaranteed
to all the people their liberties – you [Democrats] refused to
acquiesce in [agree to] the laws enacted by Congress – you
[Democrats] refused to "accept the situation" – to recognize
the rights of that class of men in the land. You sought to make
the reconstruction acts a nullity, if possible. You sought to re-
enslave the black man by every means in your power. [326]

Southern Democrats went well beyond Black Codes, however, and
also imposed forced segregation. In 1881, Tennessee became the first
State to do so, [327] and over the next decade, several other southern
States followed. [328] As a result, schools, hospitals, public transportation, and restaurants became segregated – despite federal laws to the
contrary. Those Democratic pro-segregation State laws replaced the
anti-segregation federal laws passed by Republicans in 1875 and regrettably became the legal standard for the next seventy-five years.

The sixth device to disenfranchise black voters was bizarre gerrymandering. Gerrymandering is the practice of combining enough
favorable parts of a district to give a pre-selected candidate or party
a majority of voters, thus ensuring that the opponent cannot win in
that district. Frequently, the result is an unwieldy-shaped district
that – rather than being a simple, tight, and geographically-compact
district – instead sprawls illogically, even following sidewalks or riv-
ers in an absurd effort to connect favorable neighborhoods. The first
district drawn in this manner was in Massachusetts in 1812; it was
drawn to ensure that candidate Elbridge Gerry would win that district over his challenger (hence the term "Gerry-mandering" [†]). That
practice has continued over the decades since; and when Democrats
regained State legislatures in the South at the end of Reconstruction,
they drew districts to ensure that the majority of voters were white
Democrats, thereby preventing blacks from being elected. [329] Often

---

† One observer who saw that original district drawn for Elbridge Gerry noted that its
shape resembled a salamander. An associate exclaimed, "No! It's a Gerry-mander!"

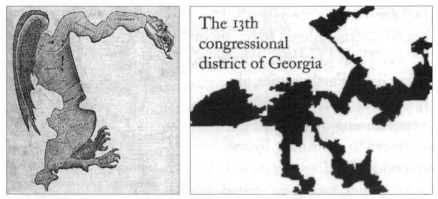

The 13th
congressional
district of Georgia

GERRYMANDERING – ORIGINAL AND MODERN

these districts would split a single black neighborhood between several different districts in order to dilute the strength of that community. This practice was extremely effective.

For example, while many blacks were elected as Republicans in Texas during Reconstruction, [330] after Reconstruction, Democrats regained the legislature and began to redraw voting lines so that when the last African American left the State House in 1897, not another one was elected – either as a Republican or a Democrat – for the next 70 years until federal courts struck down the way Texas Democrats drew voting lines. [331] Furthermore, although Republicans had been an overwhelming majority in the Texas legislature during Reconstruction, after Democrats redrew election lines, for several decades there were never more than two Republicans serving in the entire legislature at any one time. [332] This pattern was typical in other southern States as well. [333]

The seventh device used to disenfranchise black voters was that of white-only primaries. For example, Democrats in Texas enacted a State law prohibiting blacks from voting in Democratic primaries, [334] but when the U. S. Supreme Court finally struck down this statewide law in 1927, [335] the Democratic Party in Texas, [336] as well as in Georgia, [337] Louisiana, [338] Florida, [339] Mississippi, [340] South Carolina, [341] and Arkansas [342] simply enacted internal Democratic Party policies to prevent blacks from voting in Democratic primaries. And because Democrats at that time solidly controlled every level of government in the South, this Democratic Party policy had the same effect as a State law, thus ensuring that no black would be elected. In 1935, the Supreme Court upheld this Democratic Party policy, [343] but in 1944 the Court finally reversed itself and struck down white-only Democratic primaries. [344]

The eighth device used by Democrats to disenfranchise black Americans was that of physical intimidation and violence. Recall that in 1871, Rep. Rob-

ert Brown Elliott had concluded: "the declared purpose [of the Democratic Party is] to defeat the ballot with the bullet and other co-ercive means." [345] Elliott's term "co-ercive means" accu-rately described the

DEMOCRATIC VIOLENCE AGAINST BLACKS BECAME COMMONPLACE

lynchings as well as the cross burnings, church burnings, incarceration on trumped-up charges, beatings, rapes, murders, and intimidations

to which blacks in the South were subjected. Obviously, the Ku Klux Klan was a leader in this form of violent voter intimidation. As confirmed by Rep. James T. Rapier of Alabama:

> They [Democrats] were hunting me down as the partridge on the mount, night and day with their Ku Klux Klan, simply be-cause I was a Republican and refused to bow at the foot of their Baal. [346]

REP. JAMES T. RAPIER

The ninth device used by Democrats to disenfranchise black voters was the revision of State constitutions. Recall that during Reconstruction, southern States had been required to rewrite their State constitutions to add full civil rights protections for black Americans. [347] However, when those States reverted to Democratic control, many revised their constitutions to remove those civil rights clauses. For example, in 1868 North Carolina had rewritten its constitution to include civil rights, [348] but in 1876 it amended its constitution to exclude most blacks from voting. [349] Over the next two decades, Democrats in Mississippi, [350] South Carolina, [351] Louisiana, [352] Florida, [353] Alabama, [354] Texas, [355] Virginia, [356] and other southern States also altered their constitutions or passed laws to negate many of the rights that had been gained.

Other devices employed by Democrats to keep blacks from voting included property ownership requirements. For example, in Alabama in 1901, a voter was required to own land or property worth at least $300 before he could vote [357] – an amount that today would equate to more than $6,500. [358] And Florida would withhold voting rights for the "commission" of a crime – not for a serious crime or a felony but rather for violating any of a long list of petty offenses. For example, unemployed blacks looking for work were often charged with vagrancy, thus resulting in a loss of their voting rights – simply because they were looking for work! [359] Democrats also used restrictive eligibility requirements (such as residing in a State two years before voting [360]) or the paying of excessive annual voter registration fees – fees not struck down by the courts until 1971. [361]

Democrats utilized nearly a dozen devices to keep black Americans from voting – something that would have come as no surprise to the earliest African American civil rights leaders. For example, Rep. Joseph Hayne Rainey had earlier declared:

> You cannot expect the Negro to rise while the Democrats are trampling upon him and his rights. We ask you, sir, to do by the Negro as you ought to do by him in justice. If the Democrats are such staunch friends of the Negro, why is it that when propositions are offered here and elsewhere looking to the elevation of the colored race and the extension of right and justice to them, do the Democrats array themselves in unbroken phalanx [organized ranks] and vote against every such measure? [362]

Frederick Douglass agreed with Rainey and also affirmed the basic Democratic hostility for those civil rights. Douglass had explained:

> [I]n all the [southern] States, the Fourteenth and Fifteenth Amendments of the Constitution are practically of no force or effect. . . . By means of the shotgun and midnight raid, the old master class has triumphed over the newly enfranchised citizen and put the Constitution under their feet. . . . [T]he colored people, who largely outnumber the whites and who are Republican in politics, have been banished from the ballot box and robbed of representation in the councils of the nation and . . . the social condition of the colored people in that section is but little above what it was in the time of slavery. [363]

DOUGLASS FOUGHT FOR CIVIL RIGHTS AND LATER
WITNESSED THEIR VIOLATION BY DEMOCRATS

The unrelenting Democratic efforts to suppress black voting were successful. For example, in Mississippi in 1892, there were almost 70,000 more blacks than whites in the State; yet white voters outnumbered black voters by a margin of 8 to 1. [364] And in Birmingham, of the 18,000 blacks who lived in the city at the turn of the century, only 30 were eligible to vote. [365] In Texas the number of black voters fell from 100,000 to only 5,000; [366] the number of black voters in Alabama and Florida was reduced by nearly 90 percent; [367] and by the 1940s, only 5 percent of blacks in the South were registered to vote. [368] In fact, in 1965 in Selma, Alabama – a city with more black residents than white residents – the voting rolls were 99 percent white and only 1 percent black. [369] Clearly, those voter suppression efforts by Democrats were successful.

Returning to the 1800s, recall that Democrats regained partial control of Congress in 1876. That partial control continued for the next sixteen years until 1893 when Democrat Grover Cleveland was elected President and Democrats gained control of both the House and Senate;

UNDER PRESIDENT CLEVELAND, DEMOCRATS REPEALED CIVIL RIGHTS LAWS

for the first time since Abraham Lincoln, Democrats had full control of the lawmaking process. Given their new powers, what did Democrats do to assist civil rights? Nothing – not a single civil rights law was passed by Democrats during that time. In fact, Democrats immediately began repealing the civil rights laws that had not yet been struck down by the Supreme Court; they even repealed the civil rights laws protecting black voting rights as well as those punishing Klan violence. [370] In 1896, shortly after the Democrats had repealed those laws, the Supreme Court issued its *Plessey* v. *Ferguson* decision reaffirming its pro-segregation policy. [371]

By 1900, Democrats actually began actively to seek a repeal of the 14th and 15th Amendments. As Democratic Senator Ben Tillman from South Carolina explained:

> We made up our minds that the 14th and 15th Amendments to the Constitution were themselves null and void; that the [civil rights] acts of Congress . . . were null and void; that oaths required by such laws were null and void. [372]

According to prominent Democratic leader A. W. Terrell of Texas, the 15th Amendment guaranteeing black voting rights was "the political blunder of the century." [373] Democrats from both the North and the South agreed with Terrell (such as northern Democratic U. S. Rep. Bourke Cockran of New York and southern Democratic U. S. Senator John Tyler Morgan of Alabama) and were among the Democrats seeking a repeal of the 15th Amendment. [374] In fact, Democratic U. S. Senator Samuel McEnery of Louisiana even declared: "I believe . . . that not a single southern Senator would object to such a move." [375] (The southern Senators at that time were almost exclusively Democrats. [376]) Fortunately, these Democrats were unsuccessful in their efforts to repeal the 14th and 15th Amendments.

PRESIDENT TEDDY ROOSEVELT

In 1901, at the same time that Democrats were seeking to roll back the civil rights amendments to the Constitution, Republican President Teddy Roosevelt raised the ire of many Democrats by inviting Booker T. Washington to the White House. [377] Washington became the first African American to dine with a President at the White House. [378] While Booker T. Washington's wise counsel was snubbed by Democratic President Woodrow Wilson, [379] it was gladly sought by three Republican Presidents for whom he served as advisor, including William Taft, William McKinley, and Teddy Roosevelt. [380]

In 1915, the pro-Klan movie *Birth of a Nation* was released. It became a recruiting tool to help the Klan reach its peak membership of almost two million. [381] That film by D. W. Griffith – the son of a Confederate soldier – was based on a book called *The Clansman* that had been written by open racist Thomas Dixon, Jr. [382] Both Griffith and Dixon had incorporated material from Democrat Woodrow Wilson's *History of the American People*, [383] including Wilson's latent support for the Klan and its abominable practice of Southern Redemption. [384] In fact, President Woodrow

DEMOCRAT PRESIDENT WOODROW WILSON SHOWED
THIS PRO-KLAN MOVIE AT THE WHITE HOUSE

Wilson even showed this racist Klan-recruiting film at the White House – the first film ever shown at the White House. [385] Wilson also enacted pro-segregation policies within his administration; and under his tenure as President, the Democrat-controlled U. S. House passed a bill making it a felony for any black to marry a white in Washington, D. C. [386]

(By the way, much attention has been focused in the State and federal legislatures on reparations proposals [387] – that is, on the seeking of government payments to African Americans for the historical violation of their civil rights. Yet given the political history of African Americans, it might be more appropriate if those demands for reparations were made to the Democratic Party rather than to the federal or state governments.)

Returning to the historical timeline, by 1932, Republican Herbert Hoover had finished his first term as President and was running for re-election. His challenger was Democrat Franklin Delano Roosevelt.

In that election, Roosevelt – in an unusual move – invited black Americans to vote Democrat. Roosevelt understood his Party, however, and made only subtle overtures to black Americans while avoiding any overt civil rights promises. [388] So how

PRESIDENT HERBERT HOOVER

did black Americans respond to Roosevelt's invitation to join the Democrats? They printed and distributed a special handbill. [389] At the bottom, its caption read, "Who's a Democrat!" Most would assume this to be a question; however, it was not; it was a declaration rather than a question – notice the exclamation mark rather than the question mark at the end of the caption. So what statement was being made here about the Democrats?

Examine the picture: a young black boy gazing upward. At his foot is a newspaper with the title: "Lynch: 2 More in Florida." This is the only real text on the handbill, and since this piece was designed

1932 RESPONSE TO THE INVITATION FOR BLACKS TO VOTE DEMOCRATIC

specifically for the 1932 elections, that headline was intended to communicate something specific to the black Americans of that day. It did. That headline referred to two recent lynchings in Florida: those of Richard and Charles Smoke on August 28, 1931. [390] For

black Americans in that day, reminding them of lynchings was enough said about Democrats.

Of all forms of violent intimidation, lynchings were by far the most effective. Between 1882 and 1964, 4,743 individuals were lynched – 3,446 blacks and 1,297 whites. [391] Republicans often led the efforts to pass federal anti-lynching laws [392] and their platforms consistently called for a ban on lynching; [393] Democrats successfully blocked those bills and their platforms never did condemn lynchings.

One of the many Republican attempts to ban lynchings occurred in 1921 when Republican Rep. Leonidas Dyer of Missouri introduced yet another federal anti-lynching bill. It was once again stalled by Democrats, [394] and the effect of that delay was costly. The NAACP sadly reported that "since the introduction of the Dyer Anti-Lynching Bill in Congress on April 11, 1921, there have been 28 persons murdered by lynchings in the United States." [395] The Dyer bill was eventually killed by Democrats – as was every single anti-lynching bill introduced in

Congress, including those occasion-
ally introduced by a Democrat. [396] As
a result of the Democrats' obstruction
on this issue, Congress never passed
an anti-lynching bill. [397]

FILIBUSTER BLOCKS ANTI-LYNCHING BILL

House Democrats Succeed In
Preventing Debate on Measure
Until After Holidays.

1921 REPORT ON DEMOCRAT
PRO-LYNCHING FILIBUSTER

The accounts of lynchings are
not just the lore of ancient American history. Many alive today still
vividly remember those horrid occurrences, and many were personally
and directly impacted by lynchings. One such individual is the Rev.
Charles Jackson of Houston.

The Rev. Jackson is well known across the nation as one of our
most successful ministers. He was the first pastor in America – of any

REV. CHARLES "C. L." JACKSON

color – to be televised nationally from
the pulpit on a weekly basis. He also
built a large successful mega-church in
Houston: the Pleasant Grove Missionary Baptist Church with more than 5,000
families. Pastor Jackson has preached
across the world, started hundreds
of churches in America and abroad,
written more than a dozen books, and
traveled to foreign nations in company
with a U. S. President. He was also the
first black man in the modern era to be
invited to attend a service in a major white church in South Africa
and to be invited before the South African Parliament.

Despite his current renown, the Rev. Jackson's beginnings were
very humble. He was raised in east Texas, eight miles from the
nearest city. His mother would walk those eight miles into town
at the beginning of each week and would remain in town, working for one dollar a week (sometimes picking cotton, sometimes
doing housekeeping chores); and then she would walk home for

the weekends. One night, a terrified young black man came running up to their house; a mob was after him, seeking to lynch him. Pastor Jackson's grandfather grabbed his shotgun and went out on the front porch to await the mob and defend the young man. The young man tried to dissuade him, warning that if he tried to help, the mob not only would kill the young man but also would likely burn down the house on top of the family. To spare the family that was trying to help him, the young man fled into the woods; the mob soon caught and lynched him, hanging him from a bridge. Pastor Jackson's aunt was also taken by a mob, raped, and then murdered. The crowd refused to allow the family to reclaim the body. Understandably, these events etched vivid, indelible pictures in the mind of Pastor Jackson's mother who had witnessed the lynch mob and whose own sister had been raped and murdered by a mob.

Mrs. Jackson later became pregnant but did not know at that time whether her unborn child was a boy or a girl. Nevertheless, she faithfully prayed over that unborn child each day as she walked the eight miles to and from town each weekend. That unborn child for whom she faithfully prayed was the Rev. Charles Jackson.

Considering how the Rev. Jackson turned out, his mother must have prayed powerful words in those daily prayers over him – look how successful he has been and how many hundreds of thousands of lives he has touched. So what was the daily prayer that she prayed over him? She simply prayed, "Lord, if this baby be a boy, don't let him hang from a bridge." Quite a sobering prayer. And even though the father of one of Pastor Jackson's own staff members was lynched from that same bridge as recently as 1973, fortunately, the prayer prayed by Pastor Jackson's mother is no longer prayed in America today.

How has Pastor Jackson handled this incident that so early shaped his own life and that of his family? In the same way that so many others from that era – and from previous eras – handled the degradation and injuries: relying on their faith in God (which has always been at the core of the African American community), they forgave their tormentors and oppressors.

THE REV. RICHARD ALLEN

The Rev. Richard Allen provides an excellent example of this Christian spirit. He had been a slave in Delaware; and while only a boy, he was sold separately from his mother, whom he never saw again. While still a slave, Allen became a Christian and began to preach on his and neighboring plantations. He eventually obtained his freedom, served in the American Revolution, became a minister, and then founded the AME denomination. [398]

Despite the grief and tragedy that he had personally experienced in his own life, he understood that bitterness only harms one of the two parties involved; and quite frankly, it harms the innocent party rather than the guilty one. Therefore, Rev. Allen wisely admonished those who had been mistreated:

> [L]et no rancor or ill-will lodge in your [heart] for any bad treatment you may have received from any. If you do, you transgress against God, Who will not hold you guiltless. He would not suffer it even in His beloved people Israel; and you think He will allow it unto us? . . . I am sorry to say that too many think more of the evil than of the good they have received. [399]

The Rev. Jackson – like so many black Americans before and after him – followed the teachings of Christianity and forgave his persecutors, holding no bitterness or ill-will – even to this day. Many today are unaware of how much pain there was and how real lynching was in recent generations – generations still alive.

Recall from the lynching numbers that even though almost 5,000 Americans were lynched, black Americans were lynched at a rate almost three times higher than whites. Why? According to Rep. John Roy Lynch:

> More colored than white men are thus persecuted simply because they constitute in larger numbers the opposition to the Democratic Party. [400]

Rep. Richard Cain agreed:

> The bad blood of the South comes because the Negroes are Republicans. If they would only cease to be Republicans and vote the straight-out Democratic ticket there would be no trouble. Then the bad blood would sink entirely out of sight. [401]

REP. RICHARD CAIN

While the opposition of Democrats to African Americans was vividly demonstrated by lynchings, Democratic assault went beyond lynchings and included every possible form of onslaught against civil

DEMOCRATIC PRESIDENTIAL CANDIDATE HORACE GREELEY TELLING A BLACK VOTER
THAT IF HE WILL JOIN THE DEMOCRATS, THE KLAN WILL LEAVE HIM ALONE

rights. This fact was widely known by black Americans; as confirmed by Rep. Joseph Hayne Rainey:

REP. JOSEPH H. RAINEY

> You gentlemen on [the Democratic] side of the House have voted against all the . . . amendments of the Constitution and the [civil rights] laws enforcing the same. Why did you do it? I answer, because those measures had a tendency to give to the poor Negro his just rights. . . . and give him freedom of speech, freedom of action, and the opportunity of education, that he might elevate himself to the dignity of manhood. Now you come to us and say that you are our best friends. We would that we could look upon you as such. We would that your votes as recorded . . . from day to day could only demonstrate it. But your votes, your actions, and the constant cultivation of your cherished prejudices prove to the Negroes of the entire country that the Democrats are in opposition to them; and if the Democrats could have sway [have their way], our race would have no foothold here. . . . The Democratic Party may woo us, they may court us and try to get us to worship at their shrine, but I will tell the gentleman that we are Republicans by instinct, and we will be Republicans as long as God will allow our proper senses to hold sway over us. [402]

Frederick Douglass agreed. Consequently, he strongly admonished:

FREDERICK DOUGLASS

> Each colored voter of th[e] State should say in Scripture phrase, "may my hand forget its cunning and my tongue cleave to the roof of my mouth" [Psalm 137:5-6] if ever I raise my voice or give my vote for the nominees of the Democratic Party. [403]

Given the long historical record prior to 1932 of Democrats opposing black Americans, it was amazing that in that election Roosevelt
should reach out for black votes. So the handbill – to remind black
voters of who the Democrats were
– simply reminded them of lynchings.
It is not surprising, therefore, in that
1932 presidential election, incumbent
Republican President Herbert Hoover
received more than three-fourths of
the black vote over Democratic challenger Franklin D. Roosevelt. [404] Black
Americans – being the victims of Demo-
crat-sponsored racism and segregation
– continued their loyalty to Republicans
well into the 20th century.

HOOVER RECEIVED STRONG
AFRICAN AMERICAN SUPPORT

Despite the strong and united opposition of black Americans
against him, Roosevelt narrowly won that election; and he did genu-
inely begin to try to make some changes
in the direction of his Democratic Party.
Although he could not do much for civil
rights (and in fact did not introduce any
bills to protect or promote civil rights),
he did create what became known as
his "Black Cabinet" to advise him on
issues of importance to black Americans. [405] And it was under Roosevelt that
Democrats – for the first time – placed
language in their platform calling for an
end to racial discrimination; [406] however,
despite the new language in their plat-

PRESIDENT FRANKLIN ROOSEVELT

form, Democrats in Congress still killed every piece of civil rights
legislation introduced in that era.

A Democratic leader much more courageous than Franklin Roosevelt was President Harry S. Truman – perhaps the first national

Democratic leader to advocate vigorously for strong civil rights protections. [407] In fact, even though Truman issued an order desegregating the military, Truman learned – like FDR before him – that it was difficult for rank-and-file Democrats to reshape their long-held views on race. The depth of this Democratic opposition was apparent in Texas; when Democratic candidate for governor, Ma Ferguson, dared to criticize the Klan's role in the southern Democratic Party, she was directly opposed in the Democratic primary with a Klan candidate, thus costing her the widespread cohesive support of the Texas Democratic Party. [408] And when Democrat George Wallace ran for

governor in Alabama, he initially refused the Klan endorsement and lost the race. On his next attempt, he adopted a white-supremacy position and was elected governor. [409] So close was the affiliation between the Klan and Democrats that a number of Klansmen ran on various Democratic tickets in that era and were elected. [410] At the national level, several Democratic U. S. Senators – both early [411] and recent [412] – were members of the

KLAN PARADE IN WASHINGTON
INVOLVING DEMOCRATIC MEMBERS OF CONGRESS

Klan and wore its white hood and robe. (And in more modern times, Klansman David Duke began his career in Louisiana as a Democrat and later switched to the Republican Party; but in recent years as the Republicans in Louisiana have run candidates of color, Duke has returned to helping Democrats and opposing Republicans. [413])

Despite the existence of the Klan and other racist groups within the Democratic Party, Truman worked boldly and openly to change

TRUMAN WAS THE FIRST
DEMOCRATIC PRESIDENT TO MAKE
BOLD CIVIL RIGHTS PROPOSALS

his party. In 1946, he became the first modern President to institute a comprehensive review of race relations – and not surprisingly, he faced strenuous opposition from within his own party. [414] In fact, Democratic Senator Theodore Bilbo of Mississippi called on every "red blooded Anglo Saxon man in Mississippi to resort to any means" to keep blacks from voting. [415] But Truman continued to push forward, and he introduced an aggressive 10-point civil rights legislative package that included an anti-lynching law, a ban on the poll tax, and desegregation of the military; but Democrats – again – killed all of his proposals, including his proposed Civil Rights Commission. [416]

Southern Democratic governors, fearing that Truman might eventually succeed in his civil rights goals, denounced his agenda and pro-

DEMOCRATIC GOV. STROM THURMOND

posed a meeting in Florida of what they called a "southern conference of _true_ Democrats" to plan their strategy to halt civil rights progress. [417] That summer at the Democratic National Convention when Truman placed strong pro-civil rights language in the national Democratic platform, the result was a walkout of southern delegates. Southern Democrats then formed the Dixiecrat Party and ran South Carolina Democratic Governor Strom Thurmond as their candidate for President. [418] Thurmond's bid was unsuccessful.

REPUBLICAN SENATOR STROM THURMOND HIRED
TOM MOSS, THE FIRST AFRICAN AMERICAN TO SERVE
IN THE OFFICE OF A SOUTHERN SENATOR

(Thurmond later had a dramatic change of heart on civil rights issues, and in 1964 he left the Democratic Party. In 1971, as a Republican U. S. Senator, Thurmond became the first southern Senator to hire a black in his senatorial office [419] – something no southern Democrat in the Senate had ever done.)

Truman's civil rights efforts were significant; [420] and the website for the Democratic National Committee properly acknowledges Truman's important contributions. In fact, in their section called "A Brief History of the Democratic Party," Democrats declare: "With the election of Harry Truman, Democrats began the fight to bring down the barriers of race and gender." [421] Notice the word "began." That is an accurate description; starting with Harry Truman, Democrats *began* – that is, they made their *first* serious efforts – to fight against the barriers of race; yet, as already noted, Truman's efforts were largely unsuccessful because of his own Democratic Party.

DEMOCRATIC NATIONAL COMMITTEE

about the dnc   en español   contact us   privacy policy   press room   site map   Search:

GET INVOLVED   LOGIN   **BRIEF HISTORY OF THE**
Sign up for DNC email updates and   **DEMOCRATIC PARTY**
action alerts.

With the election of Harry Truman, Democrats began the fight to bring down the final barriers of race and gender. Truman integrated the military and oversaw the reconstruction of Europe by establishing the Marshall Plan and the North Atlantic Treaty Organization. Truman's leadership paved the way for civil rights leaders who followed.

THE DNC WEBSITE ACNOWLEDGES THAT FOR DEMOCRATS,
IT WAS TRUMAN WHO BEGAN THE CHANGE

Look a little more closely at the Democrats' own history of their Party. On their official website, after noting that, "Thomas Jefferson founded the Democratic Party in 1792," they list a number of years highlighting significant Democratic achievements: 1798, 1800, 1808, 1812, 1816, 1824, 1828, 1832, 1844, and 1848 – a long flurry of Democratic activity. Yet after 1848, what is the next date mentioned? It skips from 1848 to the beginning of the next century. [422] Why would Democrats skip over their own history from 1848 to 1900? Perhaps because it's not the kind of civil rights history they want to talk about – perhaps because it is not the kind of civil rights history they want to have on their website. The Democrat's website is accurate when it says that the Democratic efforts for civil rights "began" with Truman in 1946, for there certainly is much about civil rights that they would rather *not* talk about before that time.

Thomas Jefferson founded the Democratic Party in 1792 as a congressional caucus to fight for the Bill of Rights and against the elitist Federalist Party. In 1798 the "party of the common man" was officially named the Democratic-Republican Party and in 1800 elected Jefferson as the first Democratic President of the United States. Jefferson served two distinguished terms and was followed by James Madison in 1808 Madison strengthened America's armed forces -- helping reaffirm American independence by defeating the British in the War of 1812. James Monroe was elected president in 1816 and led the nation through a time commonly known as "The Era of Good Feeling" in which Democratic-Republicans served with little opposition.

The election of John Quincy Adams in 1824 was highly contested and led to a four-way split among Democratic-Republicans. A result of the split was the emergence of Andrew Jackson as a national leader. The war hero, generally considered -- along with Jefferson -- one of the founding fathers of the Democratic Party, organized his supporters to a degree unprecedented in American history. The Jacksonian Democrats created the national convention process, the party platform, and reunified the Democratic Party with Jackson's victories in 1828 and 1832. The Party held its first National Convention in 1832 and nominated President Jackson for his second term. In 1844 the National Convention simplified the Party's name to the Democratic Party.

In 1848 the National Convention established the Democratic National Committee, now the longest running political organization in the world. The Convention charged the DNC with the responsibility of promoting "the Democratic cause" between the conventions and preparing for the next convention.

As the 19th Century came to a close, the American electorate changed more and more rapidly. The Democratic Party embraced the immigrants who flooded into cities and industrial centers, built a political base by bringing them into the American mainstream, and helped create the most powerful economic engine in history. Democratic Party leader William Jennings Bryan led a movement of agrarian reformers and supported the right of women's suffrage, the progressive graduated income tax and the direct election of Senators. As America entered the 20th Century, the Democratic Party became dominant in local urban politics.

THE DEMOCRATIC PARTY WEBSITE CONVENIENTLY OMITS NEARLY HALF-A-CENTURY OF ITS HISTORY

The President following Democrat Harry Truman was World War II hero Republican Dwight D. Eisenhower, elected in 1952. Eisenhower was well aware of the southern Democratic congressional commitment to racial segregation. Understanding that it would be difficult to make substantial changes in law, and that the progress would be slow at best, Eisenhower determined to eliminate racial discrimination in all areas under his authority. He therefore issued executive orders halting segregation in the District of Columbia and federal agencies. [423] Furthermore, he was the first President to appoint a black American – Frederic Morrow – to an executive position on the White House staff; [424] and although he also proposed a vigorous civil rights legislative protection plan for blacks in the southern Democratic States, [425] Democrats in Congress were able to prevent any legislative progress. Given his pro-civil rights record, it is not surprising that in his 1956 reelection, Eisenhower – like Republican Presidents before him – received significant support from black voters. [426]

REPUBLICAN PRESIDENT DWIGHT D. EISENHOWER WITH FREDERIC MORROW – THE FIRST AFRICAN AMERICAN TO SERVE ON THE EXECUTIVE STAFF OF THE WHITE HOUSE

PRESIDENT EISENHOWER AGGRESSIVELY
PROMOTED CIVIL RIGHTS LEGISLATION

After his re-election, Eisenhower continued his civil rights efforts, but both the House and Senate were in Democratic control. In 1957, he proposed a bold civil rights bill to increase black voting rights and protections [427] – proposals promptly blocked by Democratic Senator James Eastland of Mississippi, the Chairman of the Senate Judiciary Committee. In fact, Eastland is credited with killing _every_ civil rights bill that came before his committee in the 1950s, and his committee was literally known as the burial ground for civil rights legislation in the U. S. Senate. [428] When Senate Republicans sought to keep Eisenhower's civil rights bill from going to Eastland's burial ground, only 10 Senate Democrats joined in that effort. [429] Nevertheless, those few Democrats combined with the strong Republican numbers were sufficient; they were able to prevent Eisenhower's bill from going to Eastland's committee.

With Eastland unable to kill the bill in his committee, other Senate Democrats responded with a filibuster against the civil rights bill. In fact, South Carolina's Senator Strom Thurmond, still a Democrat at that time, set the record in the U. S. Senate for the longest individual filibuster speech ever given in Senate history – over twenty-four hours of continual speaking in his attempts to block Eisenhower's 1957 Civil Rights Bill. [430] The stiff Democratic opposition in the Senate resulted in a very watered-down version of Eisenhower's original bill. [431]

Yet, despite the fact that the bill was much weaker than introduced, Eisenhower did succeed in creating a Civil Rights Division within the U. S. Justice Department, [432] as had earlier been proposed by his predecessor, President Truman. This division subsequently played a prominent role in helping secure civil rights in the South during the 1960s and 1970s. That law also started a Civil Rights Commission that became instrumental in publicizing the effects of southern segregation and racial oppression. [433]

In 1959, Eisenhower presented a second civil rights bill to Congress. That bill was met with unyielding opposition in the House by Democratic Representative Howard Smith of Virginia, Chairman of the House Rules Committee. In fact, Smith would actually disappear from Congress for weeks on end in order to keep his committee from acting on the civil rights bill. [434] But as had happened in the Senate with the earlier Eisenhower civil rights bill, a few House Democrats were willing to join with the Republicans to get that bill beyond Smith's committee. [435] Democrat Emanuel Celler of New York, Chairman of the House Judiciary Committee, exerted extraordinary effort to move the bill forward, even though he was strongly opposed by other members within his own party. [436] When the bill finally passed the House and arrived in the Senate, it was gutted by Democrats before being passed into law, once again preventing the federal government from intervening on behalf of black Americans whose civil rights were being violated in the South. [437]

When Democrat John F. Kennedy was elected President in 1960, he was less willing than Eisenhower to utilize executive orders to promote civil rights. In fact, Kennedy delayed for more than two years the signing of an executive order to integrate public housing. [438] However, following the violent racial discord in Birmingham in 1963 when Democratic Governor George Wallace prevented blacks from entering public schools, [439] Kennedy sent a major civil rights bill to Congress – a bill based on the

PRESIDENT KENNEDY WORKED FOR THE PASSAGE OF EISENHOWER'S CIVIL RIGHTS LEGISLATION

findings of Eisenhower's 1957 Civil Rights Commission. [440] Kennedy worked aggressively for the passage of that civil rights bill but was tragically assassinated before he could see its success.

PRESIDENT JOHNSON SOUGHT REPUBLICAN HELP TO ACHIEVE THE PASSAGE OF THE CIVIL RIGHTS BILLS

Kennedy's Democratic successor Lyndon Johnson picked up the civil rights measure, but like his predecessors, he faced stiff opposition from his own party. In fact, Democratic Senators Robert Byrd of West Virginia and Richard Russell of Georgia led the opposition against the 1964 Civil Rights Act, including lengthy and extended filibuster speeches. [441] Republican Senator Everett Dirksen resurrected language proposed by Eisenhower's Attorney General in 1960, thereby breaking the filibuster of the civil rights bill [442] and allowing Johnson to sign into law the Civil Rights Act of 1964, followed by the Voting Rights Act of 1965.

Perhaps the most recognizable civil rights leader of that era was the Rev. Dr. Martin Luther King, Jr. Like Frederick Douglass, the great civil rights leader of the previous century, Dr. King was also a Christian minister of the Gospel. He was with President Johnson when the famous civil rights bill was signed into law.

THE REV. DR. MARTIN LUTHER KING AND PRESIDENT JOHNSON

Though both of these important civil rights acts were signed into law under a Democratic President, it was the Republicans in Congress who made possible the passage of both acts, for Johnson had been unable to garner sufficient Democratic support to pass either bill. At that time, Democrats had 315 members in Congress, holding almost two-thirds of the House and two-thirds of the Senate. President Johnson needed only a majority – only 269 votes – to get those bills passed; but out of the 315 Democrats, only

198 voted for the Civil Rights and Voting Rights Acts. Democrats had it completely within their power to pass those bills but did not. Republicans overwhelmingly came to the aid of Democratic President Johnson: in fact, 83 percent of Republicans voted for those bills, [443] a percentage of support almost twenty points higher than that of the Democrats. [444] If had not been for the strong support of Republicans, the Civil Rights Act of 1964 and the Voting Rights Act of 1965 would never have become law – not to overlook the fact that the heart of both bills came from the work of Republican President Dwight D. Eisenhower.

Other significant progress in civil rights also occurred in 1964, for in addition to the Civil Rights Act, the 24th Amendment to the Constitution was added that year, abolishing the poll tax. Significantly, a repeal of the poll tax had been proposed on at least fourteen previous occasions, [445] and on five of those occasions the House had actually passed a ban; each time the Senate Democrats had kept the poll tax alive. [446] In fact, in 1949 when Democratic Senator Spessard Holland of Florida introduced his bill to end poll taxes as part of Truman's proposed civil rights package, it too failed. It was another thirteen years after that attempt – and nearly eighty-five years after the first modern poll tax was instituted by Democrats – before the ban on the poll tax was finally approved by the Senate. [447] Significantly, 91 percent of the Republicans in Congress voted to end the poll tax – a level of support once again much higher than that of Democrats; [448] and of the 16 Senators who wanted to keep the poll tax alive, 15 were Democrats. [449] While the 24th Amendment banned

FOR DECADES, DEMOCRATS USED THE POLL TAX
TO REDUCE THE NUMBER OF BLACK VOTERS

poll taxes, it was originally applied only to federal elections; two years later, however, in 1966, the U. S. Supreme Court finally struck down poll taxes for all elections, including State and local. [450]

The 1964 Civil Rights Act had banned discrimination in voting, public accommodations, education, federal programs, and employment. [451] The 1965 Voting Rights Act had banned literacy tests and authorized the federal government to oversee both voter registration and elections in counties that had used literacy tests. [452] Those Acts opened opportunities for black Americans that they had not enjoyed since Republicans had been in power a century before; the disenfranchisement laws and policies long enforced by southern Democratic legislatures had finally come to an end.

The positive impact of these changes was both obvious and immediate. Within a year, 450,000 new southern blacks were successfully registered to vote. [453] In Mississippi, voter registration of black Americans rose from only 5 percent in 1960 to 60 percent by 1968. And the number of blacks serving in federal and State legislatures rose from only 2 in

1965 to 160 by 1990. [454]

The Voting Rights Act literally reshaped the political landscape; it was the most significant Act since the Republican Reconstruction Acts. The fact that Republicans had made possible the passage of the 1965 Voting Rights Act would have come as no surprise to Rep. Joseph Hayne Rainey, who nearly a century earlier had declared:

We intend to continue to vote so long as the government gives us the right and necessary protection; and I know that right accorded to us now will never be withheld in the future if left to the Republican Party. [455]

[It is significant that over recent years, a popular rumor has been widely circulated across the African American community that if Republicans were elected to Congress or the presidency, they would not extend the 1965 Voting Rights Act and would, in fact, remove the right to vote from African Americans. [456] (Certain provisions in the 1965 Voting Rights Act must be periodically renewed by Congress.) Many in the African American community have believed this rumor and surveys have indicated that a belief in this rumor was a substantial cause for voting against Republicans. Even though the NAACP has condemned the long-standing report as totally false (the 15th Amendment to the Constitution guarantees African Americans the right to vote, not the Voting Rights Act), [457] it has been an effective political tool for Democrats to use against Republicans. In fact, in the 108th Congress when Republicans proposed a permanent extension of the 1965 Voting Rights Act, it was opposed by the Congressional Black Caucus (composed only of Democrats) for fear that they would lose an effective political tool against Republicans.]

As many today have lost their knowledge of the black political history known so well by previous generations of black Americans, and as black Americans have in recent decades become solidly aligned with the Democratic Party, many African Americans today have picked up the Democrats' long-standing hatred for Republicans without understanding its origins; yet the racial issues behind the generations-long Democratic hatred for Republicans is well documented.

Also well documented is the fact that African Americans made their earliest and some of their most significant political and civil rights gains while affiliated with the Republican Party – and that progress is still continuing in this generation.

Consider the Texas election in which African American Ron Kirk, former mayor of Dallas, was running for a U. S. Senate seat. When Kirk lost that election, voices across the nation asserted that the South was still too racist to elect a minority on a statewide ballot. [458] What they failed to mention was that in that same election, three African Americans _were_ elected to statewide offices on the very same statewide ballot as Kirk – but those three were elected as Republicans rather than Democrats. [459] Apparently, Texas became the first State in American history to elect three black Americans to statewide office, but since they were all Republicans, that story simply was not reported. In that same election cycle, black Americans were elected to statewide office in other States as well, including a black Lieutenant Governor in Ohio and another in Maryland – both as Republicans. [460]

An important point is illustrated by these recent elections (and by scores before them): in Democratically-controlled States, rarely are African Americans elected statewide (with the exception of U. S. Senators in Illinois and a Governor in Virginia); and most African American Democratic Members of Congress usually are elected only from mi-

REP. J. C. WATTS

nority districts – that is, Democratic districts where minority voters make the majority rather than where there is a Democratic majority of white voters. On the other hand, African American Republicans are usually elected *statewide* in Republican States, or in congressional districts with large white majorities [461] – such as when J. C. Watts was elected to Congress as a Republican in a district with only 9 percent African American voters. [462] (Notably, from 1871 to 1995, when Democrats controlled Texas politics, only four minority Democrats served in Statewide office; yet in just the ten years from 1994 to 2004 when Republicans controlled the State, seven minority Republicans have served in Statewide office.)

Perhaps this explains why Frederick Douglass, a century ago, reminded black Americans: "For colored voters, the Republican Party is the ship, all else is the sea." [463] The political history of African Americans has often proved Douglass right.

Yet no one from any background – whether political, religious, or racial – should ever love any political party above principle. Although history is clear that there have been major differences in how political parties treated black Americans, neither party is completely blameless in all of its actions – nor have all the leaders in a party always been good, or always been bad. Understanding this truth,

REP. ROBERT BROWN ELLIOTT

Rep. Robert Brown Elliott – even though he was a strong Republican leader in his day – wisely advised:

> [I am t]he slave of principles; I call no [political] party master. . . . I have ever most sincerely embraced the democratic [or representative] ideal – not, indeed, as represented or professed by any party, but according

to its real significance as transfigured in the Declaration of Independence and in the injunctions of Christianity. [464]

Elliott's admonition is wise: align with political candidates that conform to what he called "the injunctions of Christianity." Republican Frederick Douglass – who served as a minister of the Gospel – had agreed, declaring:

> I have one great political idea. . . . That idea is an old one. It is widely and generally assented to; nevertheless, it is very
>
> generally trampled upon and disregarded. The best expression of it, I have found in the Bible. It is in substance, "Righteousness exalteth a nation; sin is a reproach to any people" [Proverbs 14:34]. This constitutes my politics – the negative and positive of my politics, and the whole of my politics. . . . I

FREDERICK DOUGLASS

> feel it my duty to do all in my power to infuse this idea into the public mind, that it may speedily be recognized and practiced upon by our people. [465]

Douglass was right. Citizens must vote righteously – and this first assumes that they are voting. This responsibility to vote – and to vote righteously – has been made clear from generation to generation. One such voice heralding this responsibility was that of Charles Finney.

Finney was a famous American revivalist – a leader in the American revival movement called the Second Great Awakening. He was the president of a college that even decades before the Civil War admitted both black and white students as equals. [466] In fact, the students from the college where the Rev. Finney was president not only became some of the most active conductors of the Underground Railroad but also started several of America's black colleges and universities. [467] The Rev. Finney wisely admonished:

REV. CHARLES FINNEY

[T]he time has come that Christians must vote for honest men and take consistent ground in politics or the Lord will curse them. . . . Christians have been exceedingly guilty in this matter. But the time has come when they must act differently. . . . Christians seem to act as if they thought God did not see what they do in politics. But I tell you He does see it – and He will bless or curse this nation according to the course they [Christians] take [in politics]. [468]

So when voting, no vote should be cast solely on the basis of any party; the values of each individual candidate must be examined using the standard of Biblical righteousness cited by Frederick Douglass, the principles of Christianity as cited by Robert Brown Elliott, and an awareness that voters will answer to God for their vote, as pointed out by Charles Finney.

DR. BENJAMIN RUSH

An illustration of this important principle is seen in the life of Dr. Benjamin Rush, a signer of the Declaration who worked with the Rev. Richard Allen to found the AME church. Dr. Rush served in the administrations of three different Presidents, each of whom was from a different political party. How could he do this? What was his own party affiliation? He once explained:

I have been alternately called an Aristocrat and a Democrat. I am now neither. I am a Christ-ocrat. I believe all power . . . will always fail of producing order and happiness in the hands of man. He alone who created and redeemed man is qualified to govern him. [469]

Very simply, Benjamin Rush didn't care what a party called itself. When he found someone who stood for God's principles, he would stand with him, no matter the party. The love of correct principles – and not the love of a party – must be the key to political involvement. For this reason, Founding Father Noah Webster – the author of the famous Webster's dictionary and an anti-slavery leader in his generation – reminded voters:

> In selecting men for office, let principle be your guide. Regard not the particular sect [party] of the candidate – look to his character. . . . It is alleged by men of loose principles or defective views of the subject that religion and morality are not necessary or important qualifications for political stations. But the Scriptures teach a different doctrine. They direct [in Exodus 18:21] that rulers should be men "who rule in the fear of God, able men, such as fear God, men of truth, hating covetousness." [470]

NOAH WEBSTER

Leaders for generations have wisely recognized that the quality of government depends more upon the quality and character of leaders than upon any other factor. And they also understood that we were responsible for choosing leaders of character and righteousness. Just as Frederick Douglass reminded voters of this truth based on Proverbs 14:34, so, too, did the Rev. Francis Grimke.

Francis Grimke was born to a slave mother in 1850 in South Carolina and served as a valet in the Confederate Army until Emancipation. After the war, he attended Lincoln University, Howard University, and Princeton Theological Seminary, then became minister of the 15th Street Presbyterian Church in Washington, D. C. – the same church earlier pastured by the Rev. Henry Highland Garnet. Grimke was also one of forces behind the formation of the NAACP, and in a sermon delivered on Sunday, March 7, 1909, Rev. Grimke admonished his hearers on their civic responsibilities based on God's righteousness:

> The Stars and Stripes – the old flag – will float . . . over all these States. . . If the time ever comes when we shall go to pieces, it will . . . be . . . from inward corruption – from the disregard of right principles . . . from losing sight of the fact that "Righteousness exalteth a nation, but that sin is a reproach to any people" [Proverbs 14:34]. . . . [T]he secession of the Southern States in 1860 was a small matter with the secession of the Union itself from the great principles enunciated in the Declaration of Independence, in the Golden Rule, in the Ten Commandments, in the Sermon on the Mount. Unless we hold, and hold firmly to

REV. FRANCIS GRIMKE

> these great fundamental principles of righteousness, . . . our Union . . . will be "only a covenant with death and an agreement with hell." If it continues to exist, it will be a curse and not a blessing. [471]

What legacy of faith and politics will this generation leave for the next? Obviously, the choice is ours; but having this choice, we should heed the warning delivered to citizens in 1803 by the Rev. Matthias Burnet:

> Consider well the important trust . . . which God . . . [has] put into your hands. . . . To God and posterity you are accountable for [your rights and your rulers]. . . . Let not your children have reason to curse you for giving up those rights and prostrating those institutions which your fathers delivered to you. [472]

"Blessed is that nation whose God is the Lord."
PSALMS 33:12

"When the righteous rule, the people rejoice;
when the wicked rule, the people groan."
PROVERBS 29:2

"Righteousness exalts a nation but sin is a reproach to any people."
PROVERBS 14:34

For further information, or for the historical
video or DVD of this information, visit

www.wallbuilders.com

© 2004

Endnotes

1. African-American History, "America's Forgotten Patriots, Part 3: The Spy" (at http://afroamhistory.about.com/library/prm/blforgottenpatriots3.htm); *Dictionary of American Negro Biography*, Rayford Logan and Michael Winston, editors (New York: W.W. Norton & Company, 1982), s.v. "Armistead, James [Lafayette]."

2. *Dictionary of American Negro Biography*, s.v. "Salem, Peter."

3. African American Registry, "Peter Salem, an original patriot!" (at http://www.aaregistry.com/african_american_history/1937/Peter_Salem_an_original_patriot).

4. *Dictionary of American Negro Biography*, s.v. "Whipple, Prince" and "Cromwell, Oliver"; *Ebony Pictorial History of Black America* (Nashville: The Southwestern Company, 1971), Vol. 1, p. 85.

5. Benjamin Quarles, *The Negro in the American Revolution* (Chapel Hill: University of North Carolina Press, 1961), pp. viii-ix; Joseph T. Wilson, *The Black Phalanx* (Hartford: American Publishing Company, 1889), pp. 22-23. For additional accounts of individual soldiers and units see *African American and American Indian Patriots of the Revolutionary War* (Washington, DC: National Society Daughters of the American Revolution, 2001); William Nell, *Services of Colored Americans in the Wars of 1776 and 1812* (Boston: Robert F. Wallcut, 1852) and *The Colored Patriots of the American Revolution* (Boston: Robert F. Wallcut, 1855).

6. *Dictionary of American Negro Biography*, s.v. "Nell, William Cooper."

7. William Nell, *Services of Colored Americans in the Wars of 1776 and 1812* (Boston: Robert F. Wallcut, 1852).

8. William Nell, *The Colored Patriots of the American Revolution* (Boston: Robert F. Wallcut, 1855).

9. *Harper's Encyclopaedia of United States History*, Benson Lossing, editor (New York: Harper & Brothers, 1974), s. v. "Slavery"; W. O. Blake, *The History of Slavery and the Slave Trade* (Columbus: J. & H. Miller, 1858), p. 98.

10. Blake, *The History of Slavery and the Slave Trade*, pp. 370-371; see also Thomas R.R. Cobb, *An Inquiry into the Law of Negro Slavery* (Philadelphia: T. & J. W. Johnson & Co., 1858), Vol. I, pp. cxlvii-cxlviii; see also W. E. Burghardt DuBois, *The Suppression of the African Slave-Trade to the United States of America* (New York: Social Science Press, 1954), p. 30.

11. William Nell, *Services of Colored Americans in the Wars of 1776 and 1812* (Boston: Robert F. Wallcut, 1852), and *The Colored Patriots of the American Revolution* (Boston: Robert F. Wallcut, 1855); Carter G. Woodson, *Negro Orators and Their Orations* (Washington, DC: The Associated Pub., Inc., 1925); Benjamin Quarles, *The Negro in the American Revolution* (Chapel Hill: University of North Carolina Press, 1961) and *The Negro in the Civil War* (Boston: Little Brown and Company, 1953); Wilson, *The Black Phalanx*; Booker T. Washington, *The Story of the Negro* (New York: Doubleday, Page & Company, 1909); Edward A. Johnson, *The School History of the Negro Race in America* (Raleigh: Edwards & Broughton, 1891).

12. I Samuel 17.

13. II Samuel 11.

14. II Samuel 13-18.

15. The Advocate Online, Sandra Sobieraj, "Gore says to 'Take souls to polls,'" November 5, 2000 (at http://www.theadvocate.com/election/story.asp?StoryID=887); American Daily, LaShawn Barber, "Irreverent Reverends II," February 27, 2003 (at http://www.

americandaily.com/nucleus/plugins/print/print.php?itemid=1261); No Violence Period, Jesse Jackson, "How we respect life is the over-riding moral issue" (at http://www.swiss. ai.mit.edu/~rauch/nvp/consistent/jackson.html).

16. *Dictionary of American Negro Biography*, s.v. "Douglass, Frederick"; Frederick Douglass, *Douglass Autobiographies* (New York: The Library of America, 1996), *My Bondage and My Freedom*, p. 361.

17. *Dictionary of American Negro Biography*, s.v. "Douglass, Frederick."

18. *Dictionary of American Negro Biography*, s.v. "Douglass, Frederick"; Frederick Douglass, *Douglass Autobiographies* (New York: The Library of America, 1996), *Life and Times of Frederick Douglass*, p. 453.

19. *Dictionary of American Negro Biography*, s.v. "Douglass, Frederick"; Douglass, *My Bondage and My Freedom*, p. 392.

20. Douglass, *My Bondage and My Freedom*, pp. 392-393; *Life and Times of Frederick Douglass*, p. 705.

21. Douglass, *My Bondage and My Freedom*, pp. 391-393.

22. Frederick Douglass, *The Frederick Douglass Papers*, John Blassingame, editor (New Haven: Yale University Press, 1982), pp. 385-386, from "What to the Slave is the Fourth of July?", July 5, 1852.

23. Article 1, Section 2. "The number of Representatives shall not exceed one for every thirty thousand. . ."

24. University of Virginia Library, "Historical Census Browser" (at http://fisher.lib. virginia.edu/collections/stats/histcensus/).

25. James Madison, *The Papers of James Madison* (Washington: Langtree & O'Sullivan, 1840), Vol. 3, p. 1264, speech of Gouverneur Morris on August 8, 1787.

26. *The Records of the Federal Convention of 1787*, Max Farrand, editor (New Haven: Yale University Press, 1966), Vol. III, pp. 172, 197. The quote is paraphrased, Farrand quotes Martin's report to his legislature: "[N]o principle could justify taking slaves into computation in apportioning the number of representatives a State should have in the government. That it involved the absurdity of increasing the power of a State in making laws for freemen in proportion as the State violated the rights of freedom . . . giving representation tended to encourage the slave-trade, and to make it the interest of the States to continue that infamous traffic. That slaves could not be taken into account as men or citizens because they were not admitted to the rights of citizens, in the States which adopted or continued slavery."

27. James Madison, *The Debates in the Federal Convention of 1787 Which Framed the Constitution of the United States of America*, Gaillard Hunt and James Brown Scott, editors (New York: Oxford University Press, 1920), p. 239; *The Records of the Federal Convention of 1787*, Vol. I, p. 201.

28. Jonathan Elliot, *The Debates of the Several State Conventions on the Adoption of the Federal Constitution* (Washington: Printed for the Editor, 1836), Vol. 1, p. 363, from Luther Martin's "Letter on the Federal Convention of 1787." The quote in the text is paraphrased into the first person; the exact wording in the original is in third person and states: "If they were to be taken into account as property, it was asked what peculiar circumstance should render this property (of all others the most odious in its nature) entitled to the high privilege of conferring consequence and power in the government to its possessors, rather than any other property; and why slaves should, as property, be taken into account rather than horses, cattle, mules, or other species. . ."

29. *The Records of the Federal Convention of 1787*, Vol. I, p. 597.

30. *Dred Scott v. Sanford*, 60 U. S. 393, 572-3 (1856), Curtis, J. (dissenting); John Hancock, *Essays on the Elective Franchise; or, Who Has the Right to Vote?* (Philadelphia: Merrihew & Son, 1865), pp. 22-23; *Congressional Record, 43rd Congress, 1st Session* (Washington, DC: Government Printing Office, 1874), Vol. 2, p. 409.

31. Thomas G. West, *Principles*: Spring/Summer 1992, "Was the American Founding Unjust? The Case of Slavery" (Claremont Institute); Walter E. Williams, Creators Syndicate, Inc., May 26, 1993, "Some Fathers Fought Slavery."

32. *Public Statutes at Large of the United States*, Richard Peters, editor (Boston: Charles C. Little and James Brown, 1845), Vol. 1, pp. 50-53, 1st Congress, 1st Session, "An Act to provide for the Government of the Territory Northwest of the river Ohio," August 7, 1789.

33. Democratic National Committee, "Brief History of the Democratic Party" (at http://www.democrats.org/about/history.html).

34. *Debates and Proceedings in the Congress of the United States* (Washington: Gales and Seaton, 1849), p. 1266, 9th Congress, 2nd Session, "An act to prohibit the importation of slaves into any port or place within the jurisdiction of the United States," March 2, 1807.

35. *A Thanksgiving Sermon, Preached January 1, 1808, In St. Thomas's, or the African Episcopal Church, Philadelphia: on Account of the Abolition of the African Slave Trade;* see also Sidney Kaplan, *The Black Presence in the Era of the American Revolution 1770-1800* (Washington: New York Graphic Society, LTD, 1973), p. 92.

36. *Dictionary of American Biography*, Dumas Malone, editor (New York: Charles Scribner's Sons, 1936), Vol. XVIII, s.v. "Rush, Benjamin"; *The Constitution of the Pennsylvania Society for Promoting the Abolition of Slavery* (Philadelphia: Joseph James, 1787), p. 8; Benjamin Franklin, *The Papers of Benjamin Franklin*, William Willcox, editor (New Haven: Yale University Press, 1976), Vol. 20, pp. 155-156, letter to Richard Woodward on April 10, 1773, p. 193, letter from Benjamin Rush on May 1, 1773, and p. 314, letter to Benjamin Rush on July 14, 1773.

37. Richard Allen, *The Life Experience and Gospel Labors of Rt. Rev. Richard Allen* (New York: Abingdon Press, 1960), pp. 21, 23-24; *Dictionary of American Negro Biography*, s.v. "Allen, Richard."

38. Absalom Jones, *"A Thanksgiving Sermon"* (at http://uoregon.edu/~mjdennis/courses/history_456_absalom%20jones.htm). The text of this speech appears in Dorothy Porter, *Early Negro Writing* (Boston: Beacon Press, 1971).

39. Thomas Hudson McKee, *The National Conventions and Platforms of All Political Parties, 1789-1905* (New York: Burt Franklin, 1971), pp. 18-20; Office of the Clerk, U. S. House of Representatives online, "Party Divisions" (at http://clerk.house.gov/histHigh/Congressional_History/partyDiv.php); CNN AllPolitics.com, "Democratic Party History" (at http://www.cnn.com/ELECTION/2000/conventions/democratic/features/history/).

40. *Debates and Proceedings in the Congress of the United States*, pp. 2555-2559, 16th Congress, 1st Session, "An act to authorize the people of Missouri Territory to form a constitution and state government," approved March 6, 1820.

41. *The Hingham Patriot* (Hingham, Massachusetts), June 29, 1839, letter of John Quincy Adams to the citizens of the 12th Congressional District (reprinted in the Timothy Hughes Rare & Early Newspapers catalog number 141).

42. *Statutes at Large and Treaties of the United States of America, from December 1, 1845, to March 3, 1851*, George Minot, editor (Boston: Little, Brown and Company, 1862),

Vol. 9, pp. 462-465, 31st Congress, 1st Session, Chapter 60, September 18, 1850, "An Act to amend, and supplementary to, the Act entitled 'An Act respecting Fugitives from Justice, and Persons escaping from the Service of their Masters.'"

43. Langston Hughes, Milton Meltzer, and C. Eric Lincoln, *A Pictorial History of Blackamericans* (New York: Crown Publishers, 1983), p. 139; *Chronicle of America* (New York: Chronicle Publications), p. 340; *Ebony Pictorial History*, Vol. 1, p. 228.

44. PBS online, "Africans in America: The Compromise of 1850 and the Fugitive Slave Act" (at http://www.pbs.org/wgbh/aia/part4/4p2951.html).

45. PBS online, "Africans in America: The Compromise of 1850 and the Fugitive Slave Act" (at http://www.pbs.org/wgbh/aia/part4/4p2951.html).

46. *Statutes at Large and Treaties of the United States of America, from December 1, 1851, to March 3, 1855*, George Minot, editor (Boston: Little, Brown and Company, 1855), Vol. 10, pp. 277-290, 33rd Congress, 1st Session, Chapter 59, May 30, 1854, "An Act to Organize the Territories of Nebraska and Kansas."

47. Orville Victor, *The History, Civil Political and Military, of the Southern Rebellion* (New York: James D. Torrey, 1861), p. 20; Benson Lossing, *Our Country* (New York: James A. Bailey, 1895), Vol. 4, pp. 1390-1392, Vol. 5, pp. 1400-1401.

48. *Statutes . . . from December 1, 1851, to March 3, 1855*, Vol. 10, pp. 277-290, 33rd Congress, 1st Session, Chapter 59, May 30, 1854, "An Act to Organize the Territories of Nebraska and Kansas."

49. Eugene Smalley, *A Brief History of the Republican Party* (New York: John B. Alden, 1885), pp. 30-31.

50. McKee, *The National . . . Platforms*, pp. 97-98, Republican Platform of 1856; Smalley, *A Brief History of the Republican Party*, p. 30.

51. *Dictionary of American Biography*, s.v. "Sumner, Charles."

52. Hughes, Meltzer, and Lincoln, *A Pictorial History of Blackamericans*, p. 73.

53. *Dictionary of American Biography*, s.v. "Sumner, Charles."

54. *Chronicle of America*, p. 350; see also Secession Era Editorials Project, "Columbia, South Carolina, *South Carolinian*" (at http://history.furman.edu/~benson/docs/sccmsu56527a.htm) and "Charleston, South Carolina, *Mercury*" (at http://history.furman.edu/~benson/docs/sccmsu56528a.htm).

55. Charles Sumner, *Speech of the Hon. Charles Sumner, of Massachusetts, on the Barbarism of Slavery, Delivered in the U. S. Senate, June 4th, 1860* (San Francisco: Towne & Bacon, 1860); see also *Congressional Globe, 36th Congress, 1st Session* (Washington, DC: John C. Rives, 1860), pp. 2590-2603, June 4, 1860.

56. *Dictionary of American Biography*, s.v. "Brooks, Preston Smith."

57. *Republican Campaign Edition for the Million* (Boston: John Jewett & Co., 1856), pp. 3-8; see also McKee, *The National . . . Platforms*, pp. 97-99.

58. McKee, *The National . . . Platforms*, Democratic Platform of 1856, p. 91.

59. *Dred Scott v. Sandford*, 60 U. S. 393 (1856).

60. *Dred Scott* at 407 (1856).

61. McKee, *The National . . . Platforms*, pp. 113-116.

62. McKee, *The National . . . Platforms*, pp. 108-109.

63. *Harper's Weekly*, July 23, 1859, p. 479, from an advertisement; see also Harpweek, "The Dred Scott Decision" (at http://blackhistory.harpweek.com/7Illustrations/Slavery/DredScottAd.htm).

64. U. S. Census Bureau, "Census 2000 Profile" (at http://www.census.gov/prod/2002pubs/c2kprof00-us.pdf).

65. Centers for Disease Control and Prevention: National Center for Health Statistics, "Table 16. Legal abortions and legal abortion ratios, according to selected patient characteristics: United States, selected years 1973–99" (at http://www.cdc.gov/nchs/data/hus/tables/2003/03hus016.pdf), and "Table 5. Live births, according to detailed race and Hispanic origin of mother: United States, selected years 1970–2001" (at http://www.cdc.gov/nchs/data/hus/tables/2003/03hus005.pdf). In 1999 there were 605,970 African American live births; the abortion rate was 52.9 per 100 live births, equaling 320,558 African American abortions for the year; the CDC reported 862,000 total abortions for 1999; thus the African American abortions were 37 percent of the total. See also LifeNews.com, "Pro-Life Advocate Says Abortion Unfairly Targets the Black Community" (at http://www.lifenews.com/nat347.html).

66. See note above, for Centers for Disease Control, Table 16. Abortions in the African American community have been above 33% since 1990; in 1999 (the last year data is available) the rate was 52.9 per 100 live births.

67. Zogby International, "New Poll: Majority of Americans, Blacks, Students Pro-Life on Abortion" (at http://www.zogby.com/Soundbites/ReadClips.dbm?ID=8087).

68. For example, on Senate Roll Call #192 (May 22, 2003) on prohibiting taxpayer funded abortions in military medical facilities, 88% of Democrats supported those abortions while 90% of Republicans opposed them; on House Roll Call # 215 (May 22, 2003) on the same issue, 84% of House Democrats supported them while 76% of Republicans opposed them; on House Roll Call #362 (July 15, 2003) on not funding United Nations programs that support forced abortions, 87% of Democrats supported funding those programs while 85% of Republicans opposed them; on House Roll Call #88 (April 26, 2001) on making it a criminal offense to harm a wanted unborn child (such as in the famous Laci and Conner Peterson case), 80% of Democrats voted not to protect the unborn child from criminal attack while 87% of Republicans voted for protection; on House Roll Call #115 (May 16, 2001) on prohibiting the awarding of State Department funds to foreign groups that promote or practice abortions, 84% of Democrats supported funding those groups while 84% of Republicans opposed this funding; on House Roll Call #97 (April 17, 2002) on prohibiting secretly transporting minor girls across State lines in order to receive abortions without their parents' knowledge, 69% of Democrats voted for such abortions while 91% of Republicans voted against them; on House Roll Call #343 (July 24, 2002) on prohibiting partial birth abortions, 67% of Democrats supported those abortions while 94% of Republicans opposed them; on House Roll Call #412 (September 25, 2002) on prohibiting penalizing health care providers who refuse to perform abortions due to conscience, 78% of Democrats voted to punish those providers while 86% of Republicans voted against such punishment; on House Roll Call #173 (June 8, 1999) on prohibiting the use or development of chemical abortion pills, 82% of Democrats supported the development and use of such pills while 81% of Republicans opposed them; House Roll Call #422 (July 20, 2000) on not providing abortion coverage as part of taxpayer paid federal employee health insurance coverage, 73% of Democrats supported such taxpayer funded coverage while 84% of Republicans opposed it; on Senate Roll Call #197 (July 1, 1999) on the same issue, 91% of Democrats supported taxpayer funded abortion coverage while 84% of Republicans opposed it; on House Roll Call #318 (June 22, 2000) on providing abortions in federal prisons, 66% of Democrats supported providing such abortions while 90% of Republicans opposed them; and there are numerous other votes reflecting the same results.

69. McKee, *The National . . . Platforms*, pp. 106-119.

70. *Biographical Directory of the American Congress 1774-1927* (United States: Government Printing Office, 1928), pp. 258-264.

71. *Echoes From The South* (New York: E. B. Treat & Co., 1866), p. 59, Alabama ordinance of secession; p. 66, Virginia ordinance of secession; p. 67, Texas ordinance of secession; pp. 158, 162, speech of A. H. Stephens on April 30, 1861; pp. 116, 128-130; *The Pulpit and Rostrum: Sermons, Orations, Popular Lectures, &c.* (New York: E. D. Barker, 1862), pp. 70, 73, "Speech by Hon. Alexander H. Stephens, Vice President of the Confederate States of America, delivered at the Atheneum, Savannah, March 22, 1861"; Edward McPherson, *The Political History of the United States of America, During the Great Rebellion* (Washington, DC: Philp & Solomons, 1865), p. 15, "The Address of the people of South Carolina, assembled in Convention, to the people of the Slaveholding States of the United States"; pp. 15, 16, "Declaration of the Immediate Causes which Induce and Justify the Secession of South Carolina from the Federal Union."

72. McKee, *The National . . . Platforms*, Democratic Platform of 1864, p. 122; Charles Carleton Coffin, *Drum-Beat of the Nation* (New York: Harper & Brothers, 1888), p. 375; Peter Michie, *General McClellan* (New York: D. Appleton and Company, 1901), p. 369, letter from McClellan to President Lincoln on July 7, 1862; Thomas Rowland, *George B. McClellan and Civil War History* (Kent: Kent State University Press, 1998), p. 94; Stephen W. Sears, *George B. McClellan the Young Napoleon* (New York: Ticknor & Fields, 1988), pp. 79-80, 116-117, 326-327, 376; see also original documents in our possession, entitled "The Presidential Election. Vote For General McClellan" and *The Republican Party: Its Mission to Save the Country from the Horrors of a New Rebellion* (Chicago, 1874).

73. Stephen Hodgman, *The Nation's Sin and Punishment* (New York: American News Company, 1864), pp. 68-69; McPherson, *Political History . . . During the Great Rebellion*, p. 2; J. T. Headley, *The Great Rebellion; A History of the Civil War in the United States* (Hartford: American Publishing Company, 1866), Vol. 1, pp. 38-39; see also *Chronicle of America*, p. 361; *Secession Debated*, William Freehling and Craig Simpson, editors (New York: Oxford University Press, 1992), p. 45, Robert Toombs' speech to the Georgia Legislature, Nov. 13, 1860.

74. The Handbook of Texas Online, "Knights of the Golden Circle" (at http://www.tsha. utexas.edu/handbook/online/articles/print/KK/vbk1.html); Bartleby.com, "Columbia Encyclopedia: Knights of the Golden Circle" (at http://www.bartleby.com/65/kn/KnightsG.html).

75. For example, southerner Elizabeth van Lew was a famous spy for the Union, and Confederate General Patrick Cleburne proposed that slavery be abolished and blacks be given their freedom in exchange for military service.

76. *North County Times*, "Event Revives Historical Interest" (at http://www.nctimes. net/news/040900/mmm.html); *World Book*, "The World Book Trivia Challenge: Slavery in the United States" (at http://www2.worldbook.com/weekly quizzes/trivia quiz 061603. asp); *The Decatur Daily News*, "Rebel with a Cause" (at http://www.decaturdaily.com/decaturdaily/news/020830/rebel.shtml); LewRockwell.com, "Adopt-a-Flag" (at http://www. lewrockwell.com/orig/dieteman3.html); Virginia Division United Daughters of the Confederacy, "Thin Gray Line" (at http://vaudc.org/confed vets.html).

77. Albert Bushnell Hart, *The American Nation: A History, Slavery and Abolition* (New York: Harper & Brothers Publishers, 1906), p. 67. Other sources put the figure at 25%: see for example, University of Houston, "Digital History: African American Voices" (at http://www.digitalhistory.uh.edu/black voices/voices display.cfm?id=26) and PBS.org,

"Race – The Power of an Illusion: Interview with James O. Horton" (at http://www.pbs.
org/race/000_About/002_04-background-02-04.htm).

78. University of Virginia Library, "Historical Census Browser" (at http://fisher.lib.
virginia.edu/collections/stats/histcensus/).

79. See for example LewRockwell.com, "A Jeffersonian View of the Civil War" (at http://
www.lewrockwell.com/orig2/miller1.html) and "Genesis of the Civil War" (at http://www.
lewrockwell.com/rockwelll/civilwar.html); see also Future of Freedom Foundation, "Book Review by Richard M. Ebeling: *When in the Course of Human Events Arguing the Case for Southern
Secession*" (at http://www.fff.org/freedom/1100g.asp) and Landscape Imagery, "Articles: Crop
Influence on Human History" (at http://www.landscapeimagery.com/crops.html), etc.

80. *Echoes From The South*, p. 59, Alabama ordinance of secession; p. 66, Virginia
ordinance of secession; p. 67, Texas ordinance of secession; pp. 158, 162, speech of A. H.
Stephens on April 30, 1861; pp. 116, 128-130; *The Pulpit and Rostrum*, pp. 70, 73, "Speech
by Hon. Alexander H. Stephens, Vice President of the Confederate States of America,
delivered at the Atheneum, Savannah, March 22, 1861"; McPherson, *Political History . . .
During the Great Rebellion*, p. 15, "The Address of the people of South Carolina, assembled
in Convention, to the people of the Slaveholding States of the United States"; pp. 15, 16,
"Declaration of the Immediate Causes which Induce and Justify the Secession of South
Carolina from the Federal Union." (see fn 71)

81. *The Civil Rights Act of 1964: The Passage of the Law that Ended Racial Segregation*, Robert D. Loevy, editor (Albany: State University of New York Press, 1997), p. 15; McPherson,
Political History . . . During the Great Rebellion, p. 16; *Echoes From The South*, pp. 116, 128,
130; *Public Acts of the State of Tennessee Passed at the Extra Session of the Thirty-Third General
Assembly* (Nashville: E. G. Eastman & Co., 1861), p. 1; *Christian Science Monitor*, August
15, 1997, "Guess Who's at the Heart of the Silent Majority," Clark Kent Ervin.

82. *Statutes at Large, Treaties, and Proclamations of the United States of America, from
December 5, 1859, to March 3, 1863*, George P. Spanger, editor (Boston: Little, Brown
and Company, 1863), Vol. 15, pp. 376-378, 37th Congress, 2nd Session, Chapter 54,
April 16, 1862, "An Act for the Release of certain Persons held to Service or Labor in
the District of Columbia."

83. James D. Richardson, *A Compilation of the Messages and Papers of the Presidents, 1789-
1897* (Published by Authority of Congress, 1899), Vol. VI, pp. 157-159, proclamation by
Abraham Lincoln on January 1, 1863.

84. Douglass, *Life and Times of Frederick Douglass*, p. 792.

85. *Statutes . . . from December, 1863, to December, 1865*, Vol. 13, p. 200, 38th Congress, 1st
Session, Chapter 166, June 28, 1864, "An Act to repeal the Fugitive Slave Act of eighteen
hundred and fifty"; Vol. 13, pp. 144-145, Chapter 145, June 20, 1864, "An Act to Increase the
Pay of Soldiers in the United States Army"; and Vol. 13, pp. 507-509, 2nd Session, Chapter 90,
March 3, 1865, "An Act to establish a Bureau for the Relief of Freedmen and Refugees."

86. House of Representatives, 38th Congress, 1st Session, "A Bill to Establish a Bureau
of [Emancipation,] Freedmen's Affairs," pp. 1-6, from an original in our possession.

87. U. S. Senate Bill 145, "A Bill to equalize the pay of soldiers in the United States
army," passed June 20, 1864, from an original in our possession.

88. *Statutes . . . from December, 1863, to December, 1865*, Vol. 13, p. 200, 38th Congress,
1st Session, Chapter 166, June 28, 1864, "An Act to repeal the Fugitive Slave Act of
eighteen hundred and fifty."

89. *Congressional Globe, 38th Congress, 1st Session* (Washington, DC: Congressional Globe Office, 1864), pp. 2920, 3191. Only 2 of the 83 Democrats serving in Congress at that time voted for the repeal.

90. *Echoes From The South*, pp. 77-102; see also *The Pulpit and Rostrum*, pp. 69-70, "African Slavery, the Cornerstone of the Southern Confederacy," by Alexander Stephens, Vice President of the Confederacy.

91. *Echoes From The South*, p. 85; see also *The Pulpit and Rostrum*, p. 69, "African Slavery, the Cornerstone of the Southern Confederacy," by Alexander Stephens, Vice President of the Confederacy.

92. *Echoes From The South*, pp. 85-86; see also *The Pulpit and Rostrum*, pp. 69-70, "African Slavery, the Cornerstone of the Southern Confederacy," by Alexander Stephens, Vice President of the Confederacy.

93. *Testimony Taken by the Joint Select Committee to Inquire into the Condition of Affairs in the Late Insurrectionary States* (New York: AMS Press, 1968), Vol. III, p. 97, South Carolina, testimony by E. W. Seibels.

94. *Appletons' Cyclopaedia of American Biography*, James Wilson and John Fiske, editors (New York: D. Appleton and Company, 1888), s.v. "McClellan, George Brinton"; *Dictionary of American Biography*, s.v. "McClellan, George Brinton."

95. George McClellan, *McClellan's Own Story* (New York: Charles L. Webster & Company, 1887), p. 34; see also George McClellan, *The Civil War Papers of George B. McClellan* (New York: Ticknor & Fields, 1989), pp. 26, 128, 132. For an example of a Union General who did not return escaped slaves, see Bruce Catton, *The Coming Fury* (New York: Doubleday & Company, Inc., 1961), pp. 394-397, describing General Ben Butler's refusal to return escaped slaves.

96. Benjamin F. Cook, *History of the Twelfth Massachusetts Volunteers* (Boston: Twelfth Regiment Association, 1882), pp. 21-24; *The Annals of America* (Chicago: Encyclopedia Britannica, 1968), p. 145. Alexander Autographs sold at auction on April 2, 2003, item 554 to the author, a group of documents about the "Organization of the Webster Regiment" with this description: "Organized by Daniel Webster's son, the members of the regiment considered their role to be one of abolition and thus the regiment was destined to become one of the hardest fighting regiments in the war."

97. Benson Lossing, *Harper's Popular Cyclopaedia of United States History* (New York: Harper & Brothers, 1889), s.v. "Antietam Creek"; *Dictionary Of American History*, James Truslow Adams, editor (New York: Charles Scribner's Sons, 1940), s.v. "Antietam, The Battle of"; Carman Geneology Home Page, "Battle Hymn" (at http://www.carman.net/battlehymn.htm).

98. From an original 1864 document in our possession, entitled "The Presidential Election. Vote For General McClellan."

99. From an original 1864 document in our possession, entitled "The Presidential Election. Vote For General McClellan."

100. Douglass, *The Frederick Douglass Papers*, Vol. 4, p. 12, "The Mission of the War: An Address Delivered in New York, New York, on 13 January 1864."

101. McKee, *The National . . . Platforms*, p. 125, Republican Platform of 1864; also from an original 1864 broadside platform in our possession.

102. *A Documentary History of the Negro People in the United States* (New York: Citadel Press, 1990), Vol. I, pp. 489-490, "Negro Fighters for Freedom and Unity, 1863-1865," taken from J. J. Hill, *A Sketch of the 29th Regiment of Connecticut Colored Troops* (Baltimore, 1867), pp. 25-27.

103. From a letter written by Mrs. Caroline Johnson and sold at auction by Historical Collection Auctions on November 6th, 2003; a copy of the letter is in our possession.

104. The Harris Poll #11, February 26, 2003, "The Religious and Other Beliefs of Americans 2003" (at http://www.harrisinteractive.com/harris_poll/printerfriend/index.asp?PID=359); see also a recent Barna poll (at http://www.barna.org/cgi-bin/PageCategory.asp?CategoryID=1).

105. *Congressional Globe, 38th Congress, 1st Session* (Washington, DC: Congressional Globe Office, 1864), p. 1490, April 8, 1864; *Congressional Globe, 38th Congress, 2nd Session* (Washington, DC: Congressional Globe Office, 1865), pp. 523-531, January 31, 1865.

106. From an original in our possession: "Photo collage of the members of Congress who signed the 13th Amendment."

107. *Journal of the House of Representatives, 38th Congress, 2nd Session* (Washington: Government Printing Office, 1865), pp. 168-171, January 31, 1865; *Journal of the Senate, 38th Congress, 1st Session* (Washington: Government Printing Office, 1863), p. 313, April 11, 1864.

108. *Congressional Globe, 38th Congress, 2nd Session* (Washington, DC: Congressional Globe Office, 1865), p. 532, February 1, 1865; U. S. National Archives & Records Administration, "The Constitutional Amendment Process" (at http://www.archives.gov/federal_register/constitution/amendment_process.html).

109. *Debates and Proceedings in the Congress of the United States*, p. 797, December 4, 1800, 6th Congress; see also Charles Lanman, *Dictionary of the United States Congress* (Hartford: T. Belknap and H. E. Goodwin, 1868), p. 438.

110. James Hutson, *Religion and the Founding of the American Republic* (Washington, DC: Library of Congress, 1998), p. 91.

111. Henry Highland Garnet, *Memorial Discourse* (Philadelphia: Joseph M. Wilson, 1865), p. 73.

112. Garnet, *Memorial Discourse*, pp. 80, 81, 82.

113. Garnet, *Memorial Discourse*, pp. 85, 88, 89.

114. Garnet, *Memorial Discourse*, p. 16.

115. The Gallup Organization, "Most Americans Support Prayer in Public Schools" (at http://www.gallup.com/content/login.aspx?ci=3730); CNN.com, "N. Texas School Administrators to Comply with Supreme Court Ruling on Student Prayer" (at http://www.cnn.com/2000/LOCAL/southwest/06/20/ftw.schoolprayer/index.html).

116. H J RES 78, House Roll Call #201 on June 4, 1998 (at http://clerk.house.gov/evs/1998/roll201.xml).

117. National Constitution Center, "Gallup and National Constitution Center Collaborate on Poll, Other Civic Projects: 2003 Talk Back Study" (at http://www.constitutioncenter.org/PressRoom/PressReleases/2003_12_18_3669.shtml).

118. H R 1501, House Roll Call #221 on June 17, 1999 (at http://clerk.house.gov/evs/1999/roll221.xml).

119. H R 235, "Houses of Worship Free Speech Restoration Act," 108th Congress, (go to http://thomas.loc.gov and enter "HR 235").

120. H R 2357, House Roll Call #429 on October 2, 2002 (at http://clerk.house.gov/evs/2002/roll429.xml).

121. S J Res 40, Senate Roll Call #155 on July 14, 2004 (at http://www.senate.gov/legislative/LIS/roll_call_lists/roll_call_vote_cfm.cfm?congress=108&session=2&vote=00155).

122. *Dictionary of American Negro Biography*, s.v. "Rock, John Sweat."

123. *Dictionary of American Negro Biography*, s.v. "Rock, John Sweat."

124. The Handbook of Texas Online, "African Americans and Politics" (at http://www.tsha.utexas.edu/handbook/online/articles/print/AA/wmafr.html).

125. Eric Foner, *Reconstruction: America's Unfinished Revolution, 1863-1877* (New York: Harper & Row, 1988), p. 111.

126. Terry L. Seip, *The South Returns to Congress* (Baton Rouge: Louisiana State University Press, 1983), pp. 38-43; see also Page Smith, *Trial By Fire* (New York: McGraw-Hill Book Company, 1982), p. 41; House of Representatives Mis. Doc. No. 53, "Condition of Affairs in Mississippi" (40th Congress, 3rd Session, January 6, 1869), p. 265.

127. *Statutes at Large, Treaties, and Proclamations of the United States of America, from December, 1865, to March, 1867*, George P. Spanger, editor (Boston: Little, Brown and Company, 1868), Vol. 14, p. 429, 39th Congress, 2nd Session, Chapter 153, March 2, 1867, "An Act to provide for the more efficient Government of the Rebel States"; *Statutes . . . from December, 1867, to March, 1869*, Vol. 15, p. 2, 40th Congress, 1st Session, Chapter 6, March 23, 1867, "An Act supplementary to an Act entitled 'An Act to provide for the more efficient Government of the Rebel States.'"

128. Amnesty Oath, from an original in our possession that stipulates ". . . I will in like manner abide by and faithfully support all Laws and Proclamations which have been made during the existing rebellion, with reference to the emancipation of slaves."; see also *Statutes . . . from December, 1867, to March, 1869*, Vol. 15, p. 2, 40th Congress, 1st Session, Chapter 6, March 23, 1867, "An Act supplementary to an Act entitled 'An Act to provide for the more efficient Government of the Rebel States.'"

129. House of Representatives Mis. Doc. No. 53, "Condition of Affairs in Mississippi" (40th Congress, 3rd Session, January 6, 1869), pp. 9, 136, 230.

130. Foner, *Reconstruction*, pp. 313, 364; *Reconstruction and Redemption in the South*, Otto H. Olsen, editor (Baton Rouge: Louisiana State University Press, 1980), pp. 4, 121; The Handbook of Texas Online, "Reconstruction" (at http://www.tsha.utexas.edu/handbook/online/articles/view/RR/mzr1.html) and "African Americans and Politics" (at http://www.tsha.utexas.edu/handbook/online/articles/print/AA/wmafr.html); ActiveBook Experience, "Out of Many: A History of the American People" (at http://myphlip1.pearsoncmg.com/abdemo/abpage.cfm?vbcid=2743&vid=69); MSN Encarta, "Segregation in the United States" (at http://encarta.msn.com/text_761580651___3/Segregation_in_the_United_States.html).

131. The Handbook of Texas Online, "African Americans and Politics" (at http://www.tsha.utexas.edu/handbook/online/articles/print/AA/wmafr.html).

132. Hughes, Meltzer, and Lincoln, *A Pictorial History of Blackamericans*, p. 205.

133. Alabama Moments in American History, "Alabama's Black Leaders During Reconstruction" (at http://www.alabamamoments.state.al.us/sec26det.html), etc.

134. Foner, *Reconstruction*, p. 355, n15.

135. Foner, *Reconstruction*, p. 355, n15.

136. Foner, *Reconstruction*, p. 355, n15.

137. Foner, *Reconstruction*, p. 355, n15.

138. Foner, *Reconstruction*, p. 355, n15.

139. Foner, *Reconstruction*, p. 355, n15.

140. *Congressional Globe, 41st Congress, 2nd Session*, pp. 1987-1988, Hiram R. Revels addressing the Georgia Bill on March 16, 1870; see also *National Anti-Slavery Standard*, September 26, 1868, "The South. The Rebel Perfidy in the Legislature. Colored Republicans

Expelled," p. 1; and Georgia Secretary of State, "Expelled Because of their Color: African-American Legislators in Georgia" (at http://www.sos.state.ga.us/Archives/ve/1/ec1.htm).

141. *National Anti-Slavery Standard*, September 26, 1868, p. 1.

142. *Dictionary of American Negro Biography*, s.v. "Pinchback, P[inkney] B[enton] S[tewart]." Pinchback was elected president pro tempore of the state Senate and ascended to the position of Lt. Governor on the death of the incumbent; when the Reconstructionist Governor was later impeached, Pinchback assumed the duties of acting Governor until the impeachment was resolved.

143. Hughes, Meltzer, and Lincoln, *Pictorial History* (1983), p. 199; see also Harpweek, "The Impeachment of Andrew Johnson: The New Orleans Massacre" (at http://www.impeach-andrewjohnson.com/06FirstImpeachmentDiscussion s/iiib-8a.htm); *Harper's Weekly*, August 25, 1866, pp. 535-537; *Harper's Weekly*, September 1, 1866, p. 556.

144. Roger Butterfield, *The American Past* (New York: Simon and Schuster,1947), p. 222; see also House of Representatives Report No. 16, "New Orleans Riots" (39th Congress, 2nd Session, February 11, 1867), containing testimony from the congressional investigation of those riots.

145. Foner, *Reconstruction*, pp. 32-33, New York; pp. 261-262, Tennessee; pp. 559-560, Mississippi. For other accounts, see the following official reports: House of Representatives Ex. Doc. No. 268, "Condition of Affairs in the Southern States, Message from the President of the United States" (42nd Congress, 2nd Session, April 19, 1872); House of Representatives Ex. Doc. No. 342, "General Orders – Reconstruction: Letter from the Secretary of War" (40th Congress, 2nd Session, July 18, 1868); Senate Mis. Doc. 82, Part 2, "In the Senate of the United States" (51st Congress, 1st Session, February 11, 1890); *The Reports of the Committees of the House of Representatives, Made During the First Session Thirty-Ninth Congress, 1865-66* (Washington: Government Printing Office, 1866); House of Representatives Report No. 265, "Vicksburgh Troubles" (43rd Congress, 2nd Session, February 27, 1875); House of Representatives Mis. Doc. No. 154, "Testimony Taken by the Sub-Committee of Elections in Louisiana" (Washington: Government Printing Office, 1870); House of Representatives Report No. 16, "New Orleans Riots" (39th Congress, 2nd Session, February 11, 1867); House of Representatives Report No. 92, "Affairs in Louisiana" (42nd Congress, 2nd Session, May 30, 1872); House of Representatives Mis. Doc. No. 52, "Condition of Affairs in Georgia" (40th Congress, 3rd Session, February 12, 1869); House of Representatives Report No. 2, "Affairs in Arkansas: Report by Mr. Poland" (Washington: Government Printing Office, 1874); and House of Representatives Mis. Doc. No. 111, "Elections in Alabama: Affidavits of Discharge from Employment" (40th Congress, 2nd Session, March 26, 1868).

146. Smalley, *A Brief History of the Republican Party*, pp. 49-50.

147. See, for example, University of Texas at Austin, "The Ancestors of George & Hazel Mullins: Democratic and Republican Parties Compete for Power" (at http://uts.cc.utexas.edu/~pmullins/chapter12.htm).

148. *Report of the Joint Select Committee to Inquire Into the Condition of Affairs in the Late Insurrectionary States* (New York: AMS Press, 1968), Vol. I; Vol. II, "North Carolina"; Vols. III, IV and V, "South Carolina"; Vols. VI and VII, "Georgia"; Vols. VIII, IX and X, "Alabama"; Vols. XI and XII, "Mississippi"; Vol. XIII, "Miscellaneous and Florida."

149. *Testimony . . . to Inquire . . . in the Late Insurrectionary States*, Vol. II, p. 220, "North Carolina"; Vol. XI, p. 286, "Mississippi"; Vol. III, pp. 26-27, Vol. IV, p. 848, "South Carolina"; Vol. IX, p. 899, "Alabama"; Vol. VII, p. 1005, "Georgia"; and Vol. XIII, p. 66, "Miscellaneous and Florida."

150. *Testimony . . . to Inquire . . . in the Late Insurrectionary States*, Vol. III, p. 97, testimony of E. W. Sweibels on June 22, 1871.

151. See, for example, *Testimony . . . to Inquire . . . in the Late Insurrectionary States*, Vol. III, pp. 326-330, "South Carolina."

152. Alan C. Collins, *The Story of American Pictures* (New York: Doubleday & Company, Inc, 1953), p. 236.

153. *Congressional Globe, 42nd Congress, 1st Session* (Washington, DC: Congressional Globe Office, 1871), p. 394, Rep. Joseph H. Rainey addressing the bill to enforce the Fourteenth Amendment, April 1, 1871.

154. *Testimony . . . to Inquire . . . in the Late Insurrectionary States*, Vol. IV, pp. 620-623, 625, "South Carolina."

155. From an original in our possession: "Radical Members of the So. Ca. Legislature"; see also Hughes, Meltzer, and Lincoln, *A Pictorial History of Blackamericans*, p. 204.

156. The Handbook of Texas Online, "African Americans and Politics" (at http://www.tsha.utexas.edu/handbook/online/articles/print/AA/wmafr.html), and "Reconstruction" (at http://www.tsha.utexas.edu/handbook/online/articles/view/RR/mzr1.html).

157. *Journal of the House of Representatives of the United States of America* (Washington: Government Printing Office, 1866), Vol. 63, pp. 833-834, "June 13, 1866"; *Journal of the Senate of the United States of America* (Washington: Government Printing Office, 1865), Vol. 58, p. 505, "June 8, 1866."

158. From an original in our possession: "Rebel Members of the 1868 Democratic National Convention."

159. Stanley Horn, *Invisible Empire: The Story of the Ku Klux Klan 1866-1871* (New York: Gordon Press, 1972), p. 355; Smith, *Trial By Fire*, p. 924.

160. *Major Problems in the History of the American South*, Paul Escott and David Goldfield, editors (Boston: Houghton Mifflin, 1990), Vol. 2, p. 46; see also Stetson Kennedy, *After Appomattox* (Gainesville: University Press of Florida, 1995), p. 263; and Smith, *Trial By Fire*, p. 844; Francis Simkins and Robert Woody, *South Carolina During Reconstruction* (Gloucester, MA: Peter Smith, 1966), p. 566.

161. *Harper's Weekly*, October 21, 1876, p. 848.

162. House of Representatives Mis. Doc. No. 53, "Condition of Affairs in Mississippi" (40th Congress, 3rd Session, January 6, 1869), p. 146.

163. Simkins and Woody, *South Carolina During Reconstruction*, pp. 514-515; Foner, *Reconstruction*, pp. 575-575, etc.

164. *Harper's Weekly*, August 12, 1876, p. 652.

165. South Carolina, "Brief History of South Carolina" (at http://www.state.sc.us/schist.html); South Carolina Department of Archives and History, "Brief History of South Carolina" (at http://www.state.sc.us/scdah/history.htm); see also Foner, *Reconstruction*, p. 590; Ellery M. Brayton, *An Address upon the Election Law of South Carolina, and the Methods Employed to Suppress the Republican Vote* (Columbia: Wm. Sloane, 1889), pp. 15-20.

166. Manly Wade Wellman, *Giant In Gray* (New York: Charles Scribner's Sons, 1949), p. 222; see also an original pamphlet in our possession: "Rebel Members of the 1868 Democratic National Convention," p. 2.

167. McKee, *The National . . . Platforms*, p. 133, Democratic Platform of 1868.

168. McKee, *The National . . . Platforms*, p. 134, Democratic Platform of 1868.

169. From an original in our possession: "Rebel Members of the 1868 Democratic National Convention"; see also *Harper's Weekly*, February 18, 1865, p. 109.

170. Horn, *Invisible Empire*, pp. 96, 113, 254, 312; see also Kennedy, *After Appomattox*, p. 69; David Chalmers, *Hooded Americanism* (New York: Doubleday & Company, Inc., 1965), p. 20.

171. Foner, *Reconstruction*, pp. 424, 592.

172. *Statutes . . . from December, 1865, to March, 1867*, Vol. 14, pp. 428-439, 39th Congress, 2nd Session, Chapter 153, March 2, 1867, "An Act to provide for the more efficient Government of the Rebel States"; *Statutes . . . from December, 1867, to March, 1869*, Vol. 15, p. 72, 40th Congress, 2nd Session, Chapter 69, June 22, 1868, "An Act to admit the State of Arkansas to Representation in Congress"; and p. 73, Chapter 70, June 25, 1868, "An Act to admit the States of North Carolina, South Carolina, Louisiana, Georgia, Alabama, and Florida to Representation in Congress."

173. *Statutes . . . from December, 1865, to March, 1867*, Vol. 14, pp. 428-429, 39th Congress, 2nd Session, Chapter 153, March 2, 1867, "An Act to provide for the more efficient Government of the Rebel States."

174. House of Representatives Mis. Doc. No. 53, "Condition of Affairs in Mississippi" (40th Congress, 3rd Session, January 6, 1869), pp. 5, 16-17, 23-24, 51, 53-57, 94-97, 115, 143-158, etc.

175. House of Representatives Mis. Doc. No. 53, pp. 53-55, 173-174, 189-191, 204, 207.

176. House of Representatives Mis. Doc. No. 53, pp. 3, 11-12, 26-27.

177. House of Representatives Mis. Doc. No. 53, pp. 120-121, 131, 134 [troops]; pp. 157, 255, 259, 278 ["reign of terror"].

178. House of Representatives Mis. Doc. No. 53.

179. House of Representatives Mis. Doc. No. 53, p. 23.

180. University of Virginia Library, "Historical Census Browser" (at http://fisher.lib.virginia.edu/collections/stats/histcensus/).

181. *Harper's Weekly*, October 19, 1872, p. 805.

182. *The Republican Party: Its Mission* (1874), p. 10, quoting from the *Galveston News*.

183. From an original in our possession: "The First Colored Senators and Representatives"; see also Hughes, Meltzer, and Lincoln, *A Pictorial History of Blackamericans*, p. 208.

184. *Dictionary of American Negro Biography*, s. v. "Revels, Hiram Rhoades [Rhodes]."

185. *Dictionary of American Negro Biography*, s. v. "Turner, Benjamin S."

186. *Dictionary of American Negro Biography*, s. v. "DeLarge, Robert Carlos."

187. *Dictionary of American Negro Biography*, s. v. "Walls, Josiah T[homas]."

188. *Dictionary of American Negro Biography*, s. v. "Long, Jefferson Franklin"; *Black Congressmen During Reconstruction*, Stephen Middleton, editor (Westport, CT: Greenwood Press, 2002), pp. 142-143.

189. *Dictionary of American Negro Biography*, s. v. "Rainey, Joseph Hayne."

190. *Dictionary of American Negro Biography*, s. v. "Elliott, Robert Brown"; Peggy Lamson, *The Glorious Failure* (New York: W W Norton & Company, 1973), pp. 27-28.

191. *The Cleveland Leader*, February 26, 1870, Vol. XXIV, No. 4.

192. *The Cleveland Leader*, February 26, 1870, p. 1.

193. *The Cleveland Leader*, February 26, 1870, p. 1.

194. Project Gutenberg, "Ebook Speeches of the Honorable Jefferson Davis," pp. 10, 17-18, 30, 52, etc. (at http://www.gutenberg.net/cdproject/cd/etext04/sphjd10h.htm).

152 SETTING the RECORD STRAIGHT:

195. Hughes, Meltzer, and Lincoln, *Pictorial History of Blackamericans* (New York: Crown Publishers, Inc., 1983), p. 209.

196. *Congressional Globe, 41st Congress, 2nd Session,* pp. 1987-1988, Sen. Hiram R. Revels addressing the Georgia Bill, March 16, 1870.

197. *Statutes at Large and Proclamations of the United States of America, from December, 1869, to March, 1871,* George P. Sanger, editor (Boston: Little, Brown and Company, 1871), Vol. 16, pp. 363-364, 41st Congress, 2nd Session, Chapter 299, July 15, 1870, "An Act relating to the State of Georgia."

198. James Haskins, *Distinguished African American Political and Governmental Leaders* (Phoenix: Oryx Press, 1999), s. v. "Blanche Kelso Bruce."

199. Haskins, *Distinguished . . . Leaders,* pp. 23-24.

200. Biographical Directory of the United States Congress, "Rainey, Joseph Hayne" (at http://bioguide.congress.gov/scripts/biodisplay.pl?index=R000016).

201. Congressional Black Caucus, "Interactive Historical Listing of African-American Members of Congress" (at http://www.house.gov/ebjohnson/cbcformermembers.htm).

202. Black legislators who had been slaves included Senator Blanche K. Bruce (R-MS), Rep. Jefferson F. Long (R-GA), Rep. Robert B. Elliott (R-SC), Rep. Robert C. DeLarge (R-SC), Rep. Benjamin S. Turner (R-AL), Rep. Josiah T. Walls (R-FL), Rep. John R. Lynch (R-MS), Rep. Jeremiah Haralson (R-AL), Rep. John A. Hyman (R-NC), Rep. Robert Smalls (R-SC), Rep. Henry P. Cheatham (R-NC), Rep. George W. Murray (R-SC), Rep. George H. White (R-NC).

203. Congressional Black Caucus, "Interactive Historical Listing of African-American Members of Congress" (at http://www.house.gov/ebjohnson/cbcformermembers.htm); *Biographical Directory of the United States Congress 1774-1989* (United States: Government Printing Office, 1989); *Dictionary of American Negro Biography;* Haskins, *Distinguished African American Political and Governmental Leaders* (Phoenix: Oryx Press, 1999).

204. Congressional Black Caucus, "Interactive Historical Listing of African-American Members of Congress" (at http://www.house.gov/ebjohnson/cbcformermembers.htm).

205. The Handbook of Texas Online, "African Americans and Politics" (at http://www.tsha.utexas.edu/handbook/online/articles/print/AA/wmafr.html); *South Carolina v. Katzenbach,* 383 U. S. 301, 311 (1966); *Gomillion v. Lightfoot,* 364 U. S. 339, 346-348 (1960).

206. Library of Congress, *"Republican Text-Book for Colored Voters* [1901?]" (at http://memory.loc.gov/cgi-bin/query/r?ammem/murray:@field(DOCID+@lit(lcrbmrpt1615)):@@@REF).

207. *Journal of the House of Representatives of the United States* (Washington, DC: Government Printing Office, 1869), pp. 449-450, 40th Congress, 3rd Session, February 25, 1869; *Journal of the Senate of the United States* (Washington, DC: Government Printing Office, 1869), p. 361, 40th Congress, 3rd Session, February 25, 1869.

208. See, for example, the picture in *Frank Leslie's Illustrated Newspaper,* New York, April 30, 1870, p. 105.

209. *The Story of America,* Carroll C. Calkins, editor (New York: The Reader's Digest Association, 1975), p. 325.

210. *Statutes . . . from December, 1865, to March, 1867,* Vol. 14, pp. 27-30, 39th Congress, 1st Session, Chapter 31, April 9, 1866, "An Act to protect all Persons in the United States in their Civil Rights."

211. *Congressional Globe, 39th Congress, 1st Session* (Washington, DC: Congressional Globe Office, 1866), pp. 606-607, February 2, 1866; pp. 1366-1367, March 13, 1866.

212. *A Compilation of the Messages and Papers of the Presidents*, Vol. 8, pp. 3603-3611, veto message by President Andrew Johnson, March 27, 1866.

213. *Statutes . . . from December, 1865, to March, 1867*, Vol. 14, p. 50, 39th Congress, 1st Session, Chapter 86, May 21, 1866, "An Act to prevent and punish Kidnapping"; p. 236, Chapter 240, July 25, 1866, "An Act legalizing Marriages and for other Purposes in the District of Columbia."

214. *Statutes . . . from December, 1865, to March, 1867*, Vol. 14, pp. 375-376, 39th Congress, 2nd Session, Chapter 6, January 8, 1867, "An Act to regulate the elective Franchise in the District of Columbia"; pp. 379-380, Chapter 15, January 25, 1867, An Act to regulate the elective Franchise in the Territories of the United States"; pp. 391-392, Chapter 36, February 9, 1867, "An Act for the Admission of the State of Nebraska Into the Union"; pp. 428-430, Chapter 153, March 2, 1867, "An Act to provide for the more efficient Government of the Rebel States"; p. 546, Chapter 187, March 2, 1867, "An Act to abolish and forever prohibit the System of Peonage."

215. *A Compilation of the Messages and Papers of the Presidents*, Vol. 8, pp. 3670-3681, 3687-3691, 3696-3706 and Vol. 9, pp. 3707-3709, veto messages by President Andrew Johnson, January 5, January 29, and March 2, 1867.

216. *Statutes . . . from December, 1867, to March, 1869*, Vol. 15, pp. 72-73, 40th Congress, 2nd Session, Chapter 69, June 22, 1868, "An Act to admit the State of Arkansas to Representation in Congress"; pp. 73-74, Chapter 70, June 25, 1868, "An Act to admit the States of North Carolina, South Carolina, Louisiana, Georgia, Alabama, and Florida to Representation in Congress."

217. *Statutes . . . from December 1869 to March 1871*, Vol. 16, p. 3, 41st Congress, 1st Session, Chapter 3, March 18, 1869, "An Act for further Security of equal Rights in the District of Columbia."

218. *Statutes . . . from December 1869 to March 1871*, Vol. 16, pp. 62-63, 41st Congress, 2nd Session, Chapter 10, January 26, 1870, "An Act to admit the State of Virginia to Representation"; pp. 67-68, Chapter 19, February 28, 1870, "An Act to admit the State of Mississippi to Representation"; pp. 80-81, Chapter 39, March 30, 1870, "An Act to admit the State of Texas to Representation"; pp. 140-146, Chapter 114, May 31, 1870, "An Act to enforce the Right of Citizens of the United States to vote."

219. *Statutes . . . from December 1869 to March 1871*, Vol. 16, pp. 433-440, 41st Congress, 3rd Session, Chapter 99, February 28, 1871, "An Act to amend 'An Act to enforce the Right of Citizens of the United States to vote'"; Vol. 17, pp. 13-15, 42nd Congress, 1st Session, Chapter 22, April 20, 1871, "An Act to enforce the Provisions of the Fourteenth Amendment to the Constitution."

220. *Statutes at Large and Proclamations of the United States of America, from March 1871 to March 1873*, George P. Sanger, editor (Boston: Little, Brown and Company, 1873), Vol. 17, p. 601, 42nd Congress, 3rd Session, Chapter 262, March 3, 1873, "An Act to place colored Persons who enlisted in the Army on the same Footing as other Soldiers."

221. *Statutes at Large, from December, 1873, to March, 1875* (Boston: Little, Brown and Company, 1875), Vol. 18, pp. 335-337, 43rd Congress, 2nd Session, Chapter 114, March 1, 1875, "An act to protect all citizens in their civil and legal rights."

222. *Harper's Weekly*, April 28, 1866, p. 269.

223. *Congressional Globe, 42nd Congress, 1st Session* (Washington, DC: Congressional Globe Office, 1871), pp. 390-392, Rep. Robert B. Elliott addressing the Ku Klux Klan Bill, April 1, 1871.

224. *Congressional Globe,* pp. 394-395, Rep. Joseph H. Rainey, addressing the Ku Klux Klan Bill, April 1, 1871.

225. *Congressional Globe* (Appendix), p. 808, April 19, 1871; p. 831, April 20, 1871.

226. *Congressional Record, 43rd Congress, 2nd Session,* Vol. 3, pp. 956-957, Rep. Richard Cain speech on the Civil-Rights Bill, February 3, 1875.

227. Hughes, Meltzer, and Lincoln, *A Pictorial History of Blackamericans* (New York: Crown Publishers, Inc., 1983), p. 213; *Dictionary of American Negro Biography,* s. v. "Elliott, Robert Brown"; Haskins, *Distinguished . . . Leaders,* s. v. "Robert Brown Elliott."

228. *Congressional Record, 43rd Congress, 1st Session,* Vol. 2, p. 407, Rep. Robert Brown Elliott's speech on the Civil-Rights Bill, January 6, 1874.

229. *Congressional Record, 43rd Congress, 1st Session,* Vol. 2, pp. 407-410, Rep. Robert Brown Elliott's speech on the Civil-Rights Bill, January 6, 1874.

230. *African Methodist Episcopal Church Review* (Ohio: 1892) April, 1892, Vol. VIII, No. IV, p. 369, from an Article on Robert Brown Elliott by Theophilus J. Minton (at http://dbs.ohiohistory.org/africanam/det.cfm?ID2373).

231. *Congressional Record, 43rd Congress, 2nd Session,* Vol. 3, p. 947, Rep. John R. Lynch's speech on the Civil-Rights Bill, February 3, 1875.

232. *Congressional Record, 43rd Congress, 2nd Session,* Vol. 3, pp. 1011, 1870, House vote of February 4, 1875, and Senate vote of February 27, 1875.

233. *The Republican Party: Its Mission* (1874), p. 23, quoting from the *New York Tribune,* March 23, 1875.

234. House of Representatives Mis. Doc. No. 53, "Condition of Affairs in Mississippi" (40th Congress, 3rd Session, January 6, 1869), p. 24.

235. James G. Blaine, *Twenty Years of Congress* (Norwich: The Henry Bill Publishing Company, 1886), pp. 580-586; Lossing, *Our Country,* Vol. 6, pp. 1776-1781; Harpweek, "1876 Hayes vs. Tilden: Overview" (at http://elections.harpweek.com/NewSite/1876/Overview-1876-2.htm).

236. *Harper's Weekly,* September 25, 1880, p. 616.

237. Similar occurrences also took place in other States, including North Carolina and Mississippi. See, for example, *Testimony . . . to Inquire . . . in the Late Insurrectionary States,* Vol. II, pp. 95-96, 136, 168-169, 181, 225, "North Carolina"; University of Texas at Austin, "The Ancestors of George & Hazel Mullins: Democratic and Republican Parties Compete for Power" (at http://uts.cc.utexas.edu/~pmullins/chapter12.htm).

238. Rep. John Roy Lynch's speech at the 1884 Republican National Convention, p.87, from the archives of the Republican National Committee.

239. Rep. John Roy Lynch's speech at the 1884 Republican National Convention, p. 87.

240. *Harper's Weekly,* November 12, 1864, p. 725.

241. *New York Tribune,* "The Cipher Dispatches" (Chicago: Historical Society, 1879).

242. Foner, *Reconstruction,* pp. 579-580; see also Smith, *Trial By Fire,* pp. 924-925.

243. Frank Flower, *History of the Republican Party* (Springfield: Union Publishing Company, 1884), p. 332.

244. Blaine, *Twenty Years of Congress,* pp. 585, 587; Ari Hoogenboom, *The Presidency of Rutherford B. Hayes* (Lawrence: University Press of Kansas, 1988), pp. 42-49; see also Terry L. Seip, *The South Returns to Congress* (Baton Rouge: Louisiana State University Press, 1983), p. 257.

245. Seip, *The South Returns to Congress,* pp. 257-258; John R. Lynch, *The Facts of Reconstruction* (New York: Neale Publishing Company, 1913), pp. 171-181; Blaine, *Twenty Years of Congress,* pp. 595-596; Flower, *History of the Republican Party,* p. 333.

246. Harpweek, "Hayes vs. Tilden: The Electoral College Controversy of 1876-1877," Part 3 (at http://elections.harpweek.com/9Controversy/overview-controversy-3.htm), and Part 4 (at http://elections.harpweek.com/9Controversy/overview-controversy-4.htm).

247. Harvard University Press, "The Transformation of Southern Politics," from a book review of *The Rise of Southern Politics* by Earl Black and Merle Black (at http://www.hup.harvard.edu/Newsroom/pr_rise_south_repubs.html); see also *The Atlantic* online, Grover Norquist, "Is the Party Over?" (at http://www.theatlantic.com/unbound/forum/gop/norquist1.htm).

248. Digital History, "Reconstruction: Redemption" (at http://www.digitalhistory.uh.edu/database/article_display.cfm?HHID=137), "The End of Reconstruction" (at http://www.digitalhistory.uh.edu/database/article_display.cfm?HHID=138), "The Disputed Presidential Election of 1876 (at http://www.digitalhistory.uh.edu/database/article_display.cfm?HHID=139); Simkins and Woody, *South Carolina During Reconstruction*, p. 547.

249. *Dictionary of American Negro Biography*, s. v. "Walls, Josiah Thomas"; Haskins, *Distinguished . . . Leaders*, s. v. "Josiah Thomas Walls."

250. Congressional Black Caucus, "Interactive Historical Listing of African-American Members of Congress" (at http://www.house.gov/ebjohnson/cbcformermembers.htm).

251. From an original in our possession: "Politics and the School Question: Attitude of the Republican and Democratic Parties in 1876."

252. See for example, Foner, *Reconstruction*, p. 364; *Reconstruction and Redemption in the South*, p. 121; The Handbook of Texas Online, "Reconstruction" (at http://www.tsha.utexas.edu/handbook/online/articles/view/RR/mzr1.html).

253. James C. Harper, *Separate Schools for White and Colored with Equal Advantages; Mixed Schools Never!* (Washington: F. & J. Rives & Geo. A. Bailey, 1872), from an original in our possession.

254. From an original in our possession: "Tricks of the Republican Executive Committee Exposed: Ohio School System – Who are its Founders" (1875).

255. From an original in our possession: "Tricks of the Republican Executive Committee Exposed: Ohio School System – Who are its Founders" (1875).

256. Freedmen's Bureau online, "Records of the Assistant Commissioner for the State of Tennessee (at http://freedmensbureau.com/tennessee/outrages/memphisriot.htm); *Harper's Weekly*, May 26, 1866, pp. 321-322.

257. *Harper's Weekly*, May 25, 1867, pp. 321-322; Richard Bardolph, *The Negro Vanguard* (New York: Rinehart & Company, Inc., 1959), pp. 34-35, 38, 75, 105-106.

258. Foner, *Reconstruction*, p. 428; Smith, *Trial By Fire*, p. 847; see also *Congressional Globe, 42nd Congress, 1st Session*, p. 442, Rep. Benjamin Butler on the 1871 bill to enforce the Fourteenth Amendment, April 4, 1871; Africana.com, "History: Fifteenth Amendment or 15th Amendment" (at http://www.africana.com/Articles/tt_521.htm); PBS.org, "The Rise and Fall of Jim Crow: Ku Klux Klan" (at http://www.pbs.org/wnet/jimcrow/stories_org_kkk.html).

259. *Congressional Record, 43rd Congress, 2nd Session*, Vol. 3, p. 947, Rep. John R. Lynch's speech on the Civil-Rights Bill, February 3, 1875.

260. *Congressional Globe, 42nd Congress, 2nd Session*, p. 17 (Appendix), February 3, 1872.

261. *Congressional Globe, 42nd Congress, 2nd Session*, pp. 902-903, February 8, 1872.

262. *Ebony Pictorial History*, Vol. 3, pp. 124-125.

263. *Brown v. Board of Education*, 347 U. S. 483 (1954).

264. GeorgiaInfo, "The 'Southern Manifesto'" (at http://www.cviog.uga.edu/Projects/gainfo/manifesto.htm); see also *Congressional Record, 84th Congress, 2nd Session* (Washington, DC: Government Printing Office, 1956), Vol. 102, pp. 4459-4461, only 96 signers are listed on the original date of announcement: 19 Senators and 77 Representatives (others were added later); see also *Understanding the Little Rock Crisis,* Elizabeth Jacoway and C. Fred Williams, editors (Fayetteville: University of Arkansas Press, 1999), pp. 5, 16.

265. *Congressional Record, 84th Congress, 2nd Session* (Washington, DC: Government Printing Office, 1956), Vol. 102, p. 4460.

266. University of Oregon, "Breathing Spell for Adjustment Tempers Region's Feelings" (at http://www.uoregon.edu/~jbloom/race/bvbreact.htm).

267. W. Ralph Eubanks, *Ever is a Long Time* (New York: Basic Books, 2003), p. 109.

268. Texas State Library & Archives Commission, "V. McMurry to Shivers, January 10, 1955" (at http://www.tsl.state.tx.us/governors/modern/shivers-mcmurry.html).

269. Bartleby.com, "Columbia Encyclopedia: Faubus, Orval" (at http://www.bartleby.com/65/fa/Faubus-O.html).

270. Little Rock Central High 40th Anniversary, "September, 1997 – The 40th Anniversary of One of America's Most Important Civil Rights Events" (at http://www.central-high57.org/); see also *The Civil Rights Act of 1964*, p. 32; National Park Service, "Central High School" (at http://www.nps.gov/chsc).

271. *Congressional Record, 85th Congress, 1st Session* (Washington, DC: Government Printing Office, 1956), Vol. 103, p. 10771.

272. Arkansas Online, "What They're Saying About Little Rock" (at http://www.ardemgaz.com/prev/central/central0905c.html); University of Oregon, "Breathing Spell for Adjustment Tempers Region's Feelings" (at http://www.uoregon.edu/~jbloom/race/bvbreact.htm).

273. GeorgiaInfo, "This Day in Georgia History: September 4" (at http://www.cviog.uga.edu/Projects/gainfo/tdgh-sep/sep04.htm).

274. *The Journal of Negro Education,* Vol. 42, No. 1, Winter 1973, pp. 58-63, "The Segregation Academy and the Law" by Anthony Champagne.

275. *The Civil Rights Act of 1964*, p. 32.

276. Old Dominion University Libraries, "Norfolk School Desegregation: Introduction" (at http://www.lib.odu.edu/aboutlib/spccol/desegregation.shtml).

277. Louisianahistory.org, "Timeline" (at http://www.louisianahistory.org/timelines/timeline5.html); Louisiana Secretary of State, "Louisiana Governors: James Houston Davis" (at http://www.sec.state.la.us/67.htm).

278. PBS.org, "A Class Of One" (at http://www.pbs.org/newshour/bb/race_relations/jan-june97/bridges_2-18.html); Myhero.com, "Freedom Hero: Ruby Bridges" (at http://myhero.com/hero.asp?hero=rubybridges).

279. USAToday.com, "Former Georgia Gov. Lester Maddox Dead at 87," June 25, 2003 (at http://www.usatoday.com/news/washington/2003-06-25-maddox_x.htm); Bruce Galphin, *The Riddle of Lester Maddox* (Atlanta: Camelot Publishing Company, 1968), pp. 55-85.

280. Policy Review Online, "January-February 1996, Number 75" (at http://www.policyreview.org/jan96/faith.html).

281. The Citadel, "Black, White, and Olive Drab: Fort Jackson and the Civil Rights Movement in Columbia" (at http://www.citadel.edu/citadel/otherserv/hist/civilrights/papers/myers.pdf).

282. *Congressional Record, 84th Congress, 2nd Session* (Washington, DC: Government Printing Office, 1956), Vol. 102, p. 4460; William Barnard, *Dixiecrats and Democrats* (University, AL: University of Alabama Press, 1974), p. 42; Robert Garson, *The Democratic Party and the Politics of Sectionalism, 1941-1948* (Baton Rouge: Louisiana State University Press, 1974), pp. 286-287, 291-292.

283. *The Civil Rights Act of 1964*, p. 15; McPherson, *Political History . . . During the Great Rebellion*, p. 16; *Echoes From The South*, pp. 116, 128, 130; *Public Acts of the State of Tennessee* (1861), p. 1; PBS.org, "Eric Foner on the Fugitive Slave Act" (at http://www.pbs.org/wgbh/aia/part4/4i3094.html).

284. National Conference for Community and Justice, "Confederate Flag" (at http://www.nccj.org/nccj/nccj.nsf/subarticleall/352?opendocument); Factmonster.com, "Confederate Flags of the New South" (at http://www.factmonster.com/spot/confederate2.html).

285. National Center for Education Statistics, "District of Columbia" (at http://nces.ed.gov/nationsreportcard/states/ click on "District of Columbia").

286. Cato Institute, "Briefing Papers: School Choice in the District of Columbia" (at http://www.cato.org/pubs/briefs/bp-086es.html).

287. TownHall.com, Mona Charen, "D. C. vouchers," September 12, 2003 (at http://www.townhall.com/columnists/monacharen/printmc20030912.shtml).

288. Institute for Justice, "School Choice Facts" (at http://www.ij.org/cases/school/facts/dc_choice/why_dc_choice.shtml).

289. H R 2765, House Roll Call #478 on September 5, 2003 (at http://clerk.house.gov/evs/2003/roll478.xml); H R 2765, House Roll Call #490 on September 9, 2003 (at http://clerk.house.gov/evs/2003/roll490.xml); H R 2765, House Roll Call #491 on September 9, 2003 (at http://clerk.house.gov/evs/2003/roll491.xml).

290. Joint Center for Political and Economic Studies, "2002 National Opinion Poll: Education" and "1999 National Opinion Poll: Education" (at http://jointcenter.org/publications/opinion_polls.html); Public Agenda Online, "On Thin Ice" (at http://www.publicagenda.org/specials/vouchers/voucherhome.htm); see also NCPA Daily Policy Digest, "Black Parents at Odds with Black School Officials on Vouchers" (at http://www.ncpa.org/iss/edu/2002/pd022602a.html).

291. Center for Educational Reform, "Poll Finds 63% Of Americans Favor School Choice," August 20, 2002 (at http://www.edreform.com/index.cfm?fuseAction=document&documentID=956&sectionID=1).

292. *Civil Rights Cases*, 109 U. S. 3 (1883).

293. *Brown v. Board of Education*, 347 U. S. 483 (1954).

294. *Dictionary of American Negro Biography*, s. v. "Lynch, John Roy."

295. *Congressional Record, 43rd Congress, 2nd Session*, Vol. 3, p. 945, Rep. John R. Lynch's speech on the Civil-Rights Bill, February 3, 1875.

296. Haskins, *Distinguished . . . Leaders*, p. 155, s.v. "John Roy Lynch"; GOP.com, "The History Of African Americans And The Republican Party" (at http://www.rnc.org/buildingcoalitions/gophistory.htm?action=0).

297. *Official Report of the Proceedings of the Twenty-Ninth Republican National Convention* (Republican National Committee: Dulany Vernay, Inc., 1968), p. 20.

298. USAToday.com, "Conventions 2000: Rep. J.C. Watts" (at http://www.usatoday.com/community/chat/0817watts.htm).

299. TheHistoryMakers.com, "Yvonne Brathwaite Burke" (at http://www.thehistory-makers.com/biography/biography.asp?category=politicalmakers).

300. From an original in our possession: "Read Laws United States!"; citing the federal law passed on May 31, 1870, "An Act to Enforce the Rights of Citizens of the United States to Vote"; handwritten date of 1880 appears on the broadside.

301. *Dictionary of American Biography*, s.v. "Hancock, Winfield Scott"; see also The Handbook of Texas Online, "Hancock, Winfield Scott" (at http://www.tsha.utexas.edu/handbook/online/articles/view/HH/fha48.html); see also Douglass, *The Frederick Douglass Papers*, Vol. 4, p. 573, from a speech delivered at Elmira, New York, August 3rd, 1880; Smith, *Trial By Fire*, p. 799.

302. Anonymous election broadside in our possession: "Why I Will Not Vote the Democratic Ticket." 1880(?).

303. *Harper's Weekly*, November 6, 1869, pp. 712-713.

304. Foner, *Reconstruction*, p. 32; Smith, *Trial By Fire*, pp. 476-479; see also Infoplease.com, "Draft Riots" (at http://www.infoplease.com/ce6/history/A0816049.html).

305. Blaine, *Twenty Years of Congress*, p. 90.

306. Foner, *Reconstruction*, p. 588.

307. *The Republican Party: Its Mission* (1874), p. 18, quoting from the *Louisville Courier-Journal*.

308. Africana.com, "Encarta Africana: Redemption" (at http://www.africana.com/research/encarta/tt_029.asp).

309. Foner, *Reconstruction*, p. 594.

310. *Congressional Record, 43rd Congress, 2nd Session*, Vol. 3, p. 947, Rep. John R. Lynch's speech on the Civil-Rights Bill, February 3, 1875.

311. *Harper's Weekly*, October 3, 1868, p. 632.

312. Judges 16:16-21.

313. Foner, *Reconstruction*, p. 422.

314. The Handbook of Texas Online, "Constitution Proposed in 1874" (at http://www.tsha.utexas.edu/handbook/online/articles/view/CC/mhc12.html), and "Constitution of 1876" (at http://www.tsha.utexas.edu/handbook/online/articles/view/CC/mhc7.html).

315. *The Federal and State Constitutions, Colonial Charters, and Other Organic Laws of the States, Territories, and Colonies*, Francis Newton Thorpe, editor (Washington, DC: Government Printing Office, 1909), pp. 2834-2835, 1876 North Carolina Constitution, Article 5, Section 1; Article 6, Section 4.

316. Frederic Ogden, *The Poll Tax In The South* (University, AL: University of Alabama Press, 1958), pp. 2-4; House of Representatives Mis. Doc. No. 52, "Condition of Affairs in Georgia" (40th Congress, 3rd Session, February 12, 1869); Smith, *Trial By Fire*, p. 680; MyFlorida.com, "Black Judge's Honor Restored in History Books," February 27, 2002 (at http://www.myflorida.com/myflorida/governorsoffice/black_history/judge2.html); Simkins and Woody, *South Carolina During Reconstruction*, p. 550.

317. *The Civil Rights Act of 1964*, pp. 11-12; Simkins and Woody, *South Carolina During Reconstruction*, pp. 550-551; Digital History, "America in Ferment: The Tumultous 1960s" (at http://www.digitalhistory.uh.edu/database/article_display.cfm?HHID=369).

318. Digital History, "Voting Rights, Period: 1960s" (at http://www.digitalhistory.uh.edu/database/article_display.cfm?HHID=369).

319. Ohio State University, "Voting Restrictions: Jim Crow" (at http://1912.history.ohio-state.edu/race/jimcrow.htm); see also SkyMinds.net, "American Civilization: The Reconstruc-

tion" (at http://www.skyminds.net/civilization/12.php); TheHistoryMakers.com, "Timeline" (at http://www.thehistorymakers.com/historymakers/timeline/index.asp?year=1898).

320. Brayton, *Election Law of South Carolina*, p. 9; Florida: History, People & Politics, "Unit 3: Florida as a State, Civil Rights: The Case of Florida; Black Codes" (at http://www.fcim.org/flhistory/unit3_t4_case.htm); see also Woodrow Wilson, *A History of the American People* (New York: Harper & Brothers Publishers, 1902), Vol. 5, p. 137; World Socialist Web Site, "Florida's Legacy of Voter Disenfranchisement" (at http://www.wsws.org/articles/2001/apr2001/flor-a09_prn.shtml); Pensacola Beach Residents & Leaseholders Association, "Reconstruction and Revanchism in Escambia County, 1865-1888" (at http://www.pbrla.com/hxarchive_civwar_recon.html).

321. Kennedy, *After Appomattox*, p. 265; House of Representatives Mis. Doc. No. 52, "Condition of Affairs in Georgia" (40th Congress, 3rd Session, February 12, 1869); Brayton, *Election Law of South Carolina*, p. 10.

322. *Congressional Record, 43rd Congress, 1st Session*, Vol. 2, p. 408, Rep. Robert Brown Elliott's speech on the Civil Rights Bill, January 6, 1874.

323. W. E. B. DuBois, *Black Reconstruction In America* (New York: The Free Press, 1962), pp. 173, 177; *Dictionary Of American History*, s. v. "Black Codes"; African-American History on-line, "The Black Codes of 1865" (at http://afroamhistory.about.com/library/weekly/aa121900a.htm); see also The Handbook of Texas Online, "Black Codes" (at http://www.tsha.utexas.edu/handbook/online/articles/view/BB/jsb1.html); Brayton, *Election Law of South Carolina*, p. 16.

324. DuBois, *Black Reconstruction In America*, pp.172-173; Smith, *Trial By Fire*, p. 679; Brayton, *Election Law of South Carolina*, p. 16.

325. The Handbook of Texas Online, "Reconstruction" (at http://www.tsha.utexas.edu/handbook/online/articles/view/RR/mzr1.html); see also Foner, *Reconstruction*, pp. 593-594; and an original document in our possession: *The Republican Party: Its Mission to Save the Country from the Horrors of a New Rebellion* (Chicago, 1874), pp. 17-23.

326. *Congressional Record, 43rd Congress, 2nd Session*, Vol. 3, p. 956, Rep. Richard Cain's speech on the Civil Rights Bill, February 3, 1875.

327. CNN.com, "Timeline of the Civil Rights Movement, 1850-1970," February 1, 2001 (at http://www.cnn.com/fyi/interactive/specials/bhm/story/timeline.html); see also Black Voices, "Winning Civil Rights" (at http://www.blackvoices.com/feature/blk_history_98/slavery/html/2d.htm).

328. About.com, "African-American History: Creation of the Jim Crow South" (at http://afroamhistory.about.com/library/weekly/aa010201a.htm); see also National Park Service, "Jim Crow Laws" (at http://www.nps.gov/malu/documents/jim_crow_laws.htm).

329. United States Department of Justice, Civil Rights Division, Voting Section, "Introduction to Federal Voting Rights Laws" (at http://www.usdoj.gov/crt/voting/intro/intro.htm); Foner, *Reconstruction*, pp. 354, 422, 590; Woodrow Wilson, *A History of the American People*, Vol. 5, pp. 138-139; Simkins and Woody, *South Carolina During Reconstruction*, pp. 548-549.

330. The Handbook of Texas Online, "African Americans and Politics" (at http://www.tsha.utexas.edu/handbook/online/articles/print/AA/wmafr.html).

331. The Handbook of Texas Online, "African Americans and Politics" (at http://www.tsha.utexas.edu/handbook/online/articles/print/AA/wmafr.html), and "Texas Legislature" (at http://www.tsha.utexas.edu/handbook/online/articles/print/TT/mkt2.html).

332. The Handbook of Texas Online, "Texas Legislature" (at http://www.tsha.utexas.edu/handbook/online/articles/print/TT/mkt2.html).

333. Foner, *Reconstruction*, pp. 590-592.

334. The Handbook of Texas Online, "White Primary" (at http://www.tsha.utexas.edu/ handbook/online/articles/view/WW/wdw1.html). For more information see *Florida State University Law Review*, Vol. 29, 2001, "The White Primary Rulings" by Michael J. Klarman.

335. *Nixon v. Herndon*, 273 U. S. 536 (1927).

336. The Handbook of Texas Online, "White Primary" (at http://www.tsha.utexas. edu/handbook/online/articles/view/WW/wdw1.html); Texas State Library & Archives Commission, "Texas Joins The Battle: African-American Women, 1890s" (at http://www. tsl.state.tx.us/exhibits/suffrage/battle/aawomen.html).

337. Our Georgia History, "Georgia's Gilded Age: Georgia History 101" (at http:// www.ourgeorgiahistory.com/history101/gahistory09.html).

338. SSHA Political Network News, "H-Pol's Online Seminar: Historical Origins of the Runoff Primary," Fall 1996 (at http://www2.h-net.msu.edu/~pol/ssha/netnews/ f96/kousser.htm).

339. World Socialist Web Site, "Florida's Legacy of Voter Disenfranchisement" (at http://www.wsws.org/articles/2001/apr2001/flor-a09_prn.shtml).

340. Ohio State University, "Voting Restrictions: Jim Crow" (at http://1912.history. ohio-state.edu/race/jimcrow.htm).

341. StetsonKennedy.com, "*Jim Crow Guide*: Chapter 10" (at http://www.stetsonkennedy. com/jim_crow_guide/chapter10_2.htm).

342. SHG Resources, "Arkansas Timeline of State History" (at http://www.state-housegirls.net/ar/timeline).

343. *Grovey v. Townsend*, 295 U. S. 45, 55 (1935).

344. *Smith v. Allwright*, 321 U. S. 649, 658 (1944); see also The Handbook of Texas Online, "White Primary" (at http://www.tsha.utexas.edu/handbook/online/articles/ print/WW/wdw1.html).

345. *Congressional Globe, 42nd Congress, 1st Session*, p. 390, Rep. Robert B. Elliott addressing the Ku Klux Klan Bill, April 1, 1871.

346. *Congressional Record, 43rd Congress, 1st Session*, Vol. 2, p. 4785, Rep. James T. Rapier's speech on the Civil Rights Bill, June 9, 1874.

347. *Statutes . . . from December, 1865, to March, 1867*, Vol. 14, pp. 428-429, 39th Congress, 2nd Session, Chapter 153, March 2, 1867, "An Act to provide for the more efficient Government of the Rebel States."

348. *The Federal and State Constitutions*, Vol. V, pp. 2800-2803, 2814, 1868 North Carolina Constitution, "Declaration of Rights," #1, #10, #33, Article 6, Section 1.

349. *The Federal and State Constitutions*, Vol. V, pp. 2822-2823, 2834-2835, 1876 North Carolina Constitution, "Declaration of Rights," #1, #10, Article 5, Section 1; Article 6, Section 4.

350. *The Federal and State Constitutions*, pp. 2067-2068, 1832 Mississippi Constitution, Amendment 13, Article VIII; see also p. 2079, 1868 Mississippi Constitution, Article 7, Section 2; pp. 2120-2121, 1890 Mississippi Constitution, Article 12, Sections 241, 243-244.

351. *The Federal and State Constitutions*, Vol. VI, pp. 3276, 3279-3280, 1865 South Carolina Constitution, Article 4, Ordinance, Section 3; see also pp. 3281, 3297-3298, 1868 South Carolina Constitution, Article 1, Sections 1-2, Article 8, Sections 2, 12; and pp. 3307-3310, 1895 South Carolina Constitution, "Declaration of Rights," #9, "Right of Suffrage," Sec. 3 (c).

352. *The Federal and State Constitutions,* Vol. III, pp. 1449, 1462-1463, 1868 Louisiana Constitution, "Bill of Rights," #1-3, 98, 103; see also pp. 1471, 1502, 1879 Louisiana Constitution, "Bill of Rights," #5, #188; and pp. 1562-1564, 1898 Louisiana Constitution, "Bill of Rights," #197, Sections 2-4, #198.

353. *The Federal and State Constitutions,* Vol. II, pp. 704, 719-720, 1868 Florida Constitution, Article 1, 15; see also pp. 733, 747, 1885 Florida Constitution, Articles 1 & 6.

354. *The Federal and State Constitutions,* Vol. I, pp. 132, 144, 1867 Alabama Constitution, "Declaration of Rights," #1, Article 7, Section 2; see also pp. 154, 171, 1875 Alabama Constitution, "Declaration of Rights," #1, Article 8, Section 1; and pp. 209-210, 215, 1901 Alabama Constitution, "Declaration of Rights," #181, #194.

355. *The Federal and State Constitutions,* Vol. VI, pp. 3593, 3608, 1868 Texas Constitution, "Bill of Rights," Sections 12, 21, and 22, "Right of Suffrage," Article 6; see also pp. 3623, 3642, 1876 Texas Constitution, "Bill of Rights," Sections 15 and 19, "Suffrage," Article 6.

356. *The Federal and State Constitutions,* Vol. VII, pp. 3873-3875, 1870 Virginia Constitution, "Bill of Rights," #1, Article 3, Section 1; see also pp. 3904-3907, 1902 Virginia Constitution, "Bill of Rights," #1, #18-19.

357. *The Federal and State Constitutions,* Vol. I, p. 210, 1901 Alabama Constitution, Article 8, #181.

358. Columbia Journalism Review, "CJR Dollar Conversion Calculator" (at http://www.cjr.org/tools/inflation/index.asp).

359. DuBois, *Black Reconstruction In America,* p. 167; Florida: History, People & Politics, "Black Codes" (at http://www.fcim.org/flhistory/unit3_t4_case.htm).

360. Alabama Public Television, "History of the 1901 Alabama Constitution" (at http://www.aptv.org/constitution/history.html).

361. The Handbook of Texas Online, "African Americans and Politics" (at http://www.tsha.utexas.edu/handook/online/articles/view/AA/wmafr.html).

362. *Congressional Globe, 42nd Congress, 2nd Session,* p. 1442, Rep. Joseph H. Rainey's speech made in reply to an attack upon the colored state legislators of South Carolina by Representative Cox of New York, March 5, 1872.

363. Douglass, *The Frederick Douglass Papers,* Vol. 4, p. 565, from "The Lessons of Emancipation to the New Generation: An Address Delivered in Elmira, New York, on 3 August 1880."

364. University of Texas at Austin, "The Ancestors of George & Hazel Mullins: Democratic and Republican Parties Compete for Power" (at http://uts.cc.utexas.edu/~pmullins/chapter12.htm).

365. Alabama Public Television, "History of the 1901 Alabama Constitution" (at http://www.aptv.org/constitution/history.html).

366. Mike Kingston, Sam Attlesey, and Mary G. Crawford, *Political History of Texas* (Austin: Eakin Press, 1992), p. 187.

367. Alabama Public Television, "History of the 1901 Alabama Constitution" (at http://www.aptv.org/con stitution/history.html); see also World Socialist Web Site, "Florida's Legacy of Voter Disenfranchisement" (at http://www.wsws.org/articles/2001/apr2001/flor-a09.shtml).

368. Africana.com, "Encarta Africana: Fifteenth Amendment or 15th Amendment" (at http://www.africana.com/research/encarta/tt_521.asp).

369. Digital History, "Voting Rights, Period: 1960s" (at http://www.digitalhistory.uh.edu/database/article_display.cfm?HHID=369).

162 SETTING THE RECORD STRAIGHT:

370. Bernard Schwartz, *Statutory History of the United States, Civil Rights* (New York: Chelsea House Publishers, 1970), Part 1, p. 803.

371. *Plessy v. Ferguson*, 163 U. S. 537 (1896).

372. Library of Congress, "A Republican Text-Book for Colored Voters" (at http://memory.loc.gov/cgi-bin/query/r?ammem/murray:@field(DOCID+@lit(lcrbmrpt1615)):@@@REF).

373. Kingston, Attlesey, & Crawford, *Political History of Texas*, p. 186.

374. Library of Congress, "A Republican Text-Book for Colored Voters" (at http://memory.loc.gov/cgi-bin/query/r?ammem/murray:@field(DOCID+@lit(lcrbmrpt1615))):@@@REF); see also Library of Congress, "Colored Men and the Democratic Party: Review of American History on This Issue" (at http://memory.loc.gov/cgi-bin/query/r?ammem/murray:@field(FLD001+91898214+):@@@REF).

375. Library of Congress, "Colored Men and the Democratic Party" (at . http://memory.loc.gov/cgi-bin/query/r?ammem/murray:@field(FLD001+91898214+):@@@REF).

376. *Biographical Directory of the American Congress 1774-1927*, pp. 435-444, 479-488.

377. *Great Lives Observed: Booker T. Washington*, Emma Lou Thornbrough, editor (Englewood Cliffs, NJ: Prentice-Hall, Inc., 1969), p. 7; PBS.org, "The Rise and Fall of Jim Crow: The President" (at http://www.pbs.org/wnet/jimcrow/struggle_president.html); see also U. S. History.com, "Election of 1904" (at http://www.u-s-history.com/pages/h832.html).

378. Whitehousekids.gov, "Booker T. Washington" (at http://www.whitehouse.gov/kids/dreamteam/bookerwashington.html); see also *Dictionary of American Negro Biography*, s. v. "Washington, Booker T."

379. Booker T. Washington, *The Booker T. Washington Papers*, Louis Harlan and Raymond Smock, editors (Chicago: University of Illinois Press, 1982), Vol. 12, p. *xvii*, and (1977), Vol. 6, p. 548; see also PBS.org, "The Rise and Fall of Jim Crow: Booker T. Washington" (at http://www.pbs.org/wnet/jimcrow/stories_people_booker.html).

380. *Dictionary of American Negro Biography*, s. v. "Washington, Booker T."; The History of Jim Crow, "Biography: Booker T. Washington" (at http://www.jimcrowhistory.org/resources/biographies/Washington_BookerT.htm).

381. USAToday.com, "PBS Miniseries Shines Light on Reconstruction Era" (at http://www.usatoday.com/news/opinion/columnist/wickham/2004-01-06-wickham_x.htm), and "'Smile' Maligns Alma Mater" (at http://www.usatoday.com/news/opinion/editorials/2004-01-15-steiner_x.htm); Kenneth Jackson, *The Ku Klux Klan in the City 1915-1930* (Chicago: Ivan R. Dee, 1967), p. 236; Chalmers, *Hooded Americanism*, p. 291.

382. Africanamericans.com, "Birth of a Nation" (at http://www.africanamericans.com/BirthofANation.htm).

383. Woodrow Wilson, *A History of the American People* (New York: Harper & Brothers Publishers, 1902), in five volumes.

384. Woodrow Wilson, *A History of the American People*, Vol. 5, pp. 58-64, 98, 115-116, 136-137; Center for History and New Media, "The Birth of a Nation and Black Protest" (at http://chnm.gmu.edu/features/episodes/birthofanation.html).

385. Center for History and New Media, "The Birth of a Nation and Black Protest" (at http://chnm.gmu.edu/features/episodes/birthofanation.html).

386. PBS.org, "American Experience: Woodrow Wilson" (at http://www.pbs.org/wgbh/amex/wilson/portrait/wp_african.html); *Congressional Record, 62nd Congress, 3rd Session*

(Washington, DC: United States Government Printing Office, 1913), Vol. 49, p. 2920, February 10, 1913, "A bill to prohibit in the District of Columbia the Intermarriage of whites with negroes or Mongolians."

387. See, for example, H R 40 (108th U. S. Congress, 1st Session); H J R No. 25, Texas (78th Regular Session); H C R 21, Mississippi (Regular Session 2004); H R 40, Tennessee (103rd General Assembly); etc.

388. Nancy Weiss, *Farewell to the Party of Lincoln* (Princeton: Princeton University Press, 1983), pp. 100-101, 136, 139, 145, 155-158, 168, 174-179, 197-199, 209-212, 236.

389. From an original in our possession: "Who's A Democrat!" from the 1932 election, printed by the Colored Division, Republican National Committee.

390. From The Lynching Century: African Americans Who Died In Racial Violence In The United States, "The National Lists: Places" (at http://www.geocities.com/Colosseum/Basc/8507/NLPlaces1.htm).

391. University of Missouri-Kansas City: School of Law, "Lynching Statistics by Year" (at http://www.law.umkc.edu/faculty/projects/ftrials/shipp/lynchingsstate.html); see also *Negro Almanac*, Harry Ploski and James Williams, editors (Detroit: Gale Research Inc., 1989), pp. 365, 368.

392. Robert L. Zangrando, *The NAACP Crusade Against Lynching, 1909-1950* (Philadelphia: Temple University Press, 1980), pp. 16, 24-25.

393. *National Party Platforms, 1840-1976, Supplement 1980,* Donald B. Johnson, editor (Champaign-Urbana: University of Illinois Press, 1982), Republican Platforms of 1920, 1924, 1928, 1940, 1944, 1948, 1952. Cited in the American Reference Library (Orem, UT: Western Standard Publishing Company, 1998).

394. *Congressional Record, 73rd Congress, 2nd Session* (Washington, DC: United States Government Printing Office, 1934), Vol. 78, p. 11869, Rep. Emanuel Celler's speech on antilynching legislation, June 15, 1934.

395. Hughes, Meltzer, and Lincoln, *A Pictorial History of Blackamericans* (New York: Crown Publishers, Inc., 1983), p. 269.

396. *Congressional Record, 73rd Congress, 2nd Session*, Vol. 78, Part 11, pp. 11868-11869, Rep. Emanuel Celler speech on antilynching legislation, June 15, 1934.

397. History Matters, "The Body Court: Lynching in Arkansas" (at http://historymatters.gmu.edu/d/5467/); see also Bedford St. Martin's: History, "Conclusion" (at http://www.bedfordstmartins.com/history/modules/mod23/mod15_frame_conclusion.htm).

398. *Dictionary of American Negro Biography*, s. v. "Allen, Richard."

399. Allen, *The Life Experience and Gospel Labors of the Rt. Rev. Richard Allen*, p. 73, "To the People of Color."

400. Woodson, *Negro Orators and Their Orations*, p. 276, Rep. John R. Lynch from his speech in the case of his contested election.

401. *Congressional Record, 43rd Congress, 2nd Session*, Vol. 3, p. 957, Rep. Richard Cain's speech on the Civil Rights Bill, February 3, 1875.

402. *Congressional Globe, 42nd Congress, 2nd Session*, pp. 1442-1443, Rep. Joseph H. Rainey's speech made in reply to an attack upon the colored state legislators of South Carolina by Representative Cox of New York, March 5, 1872.

403. Douglass, *The Frederick Douglass Papers*, Vol. 4, p. 581, from "The Lessons of Emancipation to the New Generation: An Address Delivered in Elmira, New York, on 3 August 1880."

404. Colorado College, "A Brief History of Civil Rights in the United States of America" (at http://www2.coloradocollege.edu/Dept/PS/faculty/loevy/civil%20rights.html).

405. Hughes, Meltzer, and Lincoln, *A Pictorial History of Blackamericans*, p. 285.

406. The 1940 Democrat platform stated: "We shall continue to strive for complete legislative safeguards against discrimination in government service and benefits, and in the national defense forces. We pledge to uphold due process and the equal protection of the laws for every citizen, regardless of race, creed or color," *National Party Platforms, 1840-1976, Supplement 1980*, Donald Johnson, editor (Champaign-Urbana: University of Illinois Press, 1982). Cited in the American Reference Library (Orem, UT: Western Standard Publishing Company, 1998). Unfortunately, this language was more rhetoric than anything else since at the same time Democrats passed this language, Southern Democrats in and out of Congress were actively killing all civil rights measures.

407. Democratic National Committee, "Brief History of the Democratic Party" (at http://www.democrats.org/about/history.html). The article states, "With the election of Harry Truman, Democrats *began* the fight to bring down the final barriers of race and gender" (emphasis added).

408. The Handbook of Texas Online, "Democratic Party" (at http://www.tsha.utexas.edu/handbook/online/articles/print/DD/wad1.html); and "Women and Politics" (at http://www.tsha.utexas.edu/handbook/online/articles/print/WW/pwwzj.html).

409. Alabama Department of Archives & History, "Alabama Governors: George Corley Wallace" (at http://www.archives.state.al.us/govs_list/g_wallac.html).

410. For example, Alabama Democrats Bibb Graves was elected governor and Charles McCall was elected attorney general. See Chalmers, *Hooded Americanism*, p. 80.

411. For example, Alabama Democrats James T. Heflin was elected as a U. S. Senator, and former Klansman Hugo Black was elected as a U. S. Senator and later appointed as a Supreme Court Justice; and Texas Democrat Earle Mayfield was elected U. S. Senator. See Chalmers, *Hooded Americanism*, pp. 39, 80, 283, 305, 314.

412. NationMaster.com, "Encyclopedia: Robert Byrd" (at http://www.nationmaster.com/encyclopedia/Robert-Byrd).

413. Nationmaster.com, "Encyclopedia: David Duke" (at http://www.nationmaster.com/encyclopedia/David-Duke); TheFreeDictionary.com, "David Duke" (at http://encyclopedia.thefreedictionary.com/David%20Duke); The Hill, "Campaign 2004: State by State" (at http://www.hillnews.com/campaign/060804_state.aspx).

414. Documentary History of the Truman Presidency, "The Truman Administration's Civil Rights Program: The Report of the Committee on Civil Rights and President Truman's Message to Congress of February 2, 1948" (at http://www.lexisnexis.com/academic/2upa/Aph/truman_docs/guide_intros/tru11.htm), and "The Truman Administration's Civil Rights Program: President Truman's Attempts to Put the Principles of Racial Justice into Law, 1948-1950" (at http://www.lexisnexis.com/academic/2upa/Aph/truman_docs/guide_intros/tru12.htm).

415. Documentary History of the Truman Presidency, "The Truman Administration's Civil Rights Program: The Report of the Committee on Civil Rights and President Truman's Message to Congress of February 2, 1948 (at http://www.lexisnexis.com/academic/2upa/Aph/truman_docs/guide_intros/tru11.htm).

416. *Congressional Record, 80th Congress, 2nd Session* (Washington, DC: United States Government Printing Office, 1948), Vol. 94, pp. 927-929, February 2, 1948; see also Documentary

History of the Truman Presidency, "The Truman Administration's Civil Rights Program: President Truman's Attempts to Put the Principles of Racial Justice into Law, 1948-1950" (at http://www.lexisnexis.com/academic/2upa/Aph/truman_docs/guide_intros/t ru12.htm).

417. Documentary History of the Truman Presidency, "Attempts to Put the Principles of Racial Justice into Law" (at http://www.lexisnexis.com/academic/2upa/Aph/truman_docs/guide_intros/tru12.htm).

418. Documentary History of the Truman Presidency, "Attempts to Put the Principles of Racial Justice into Law" (at http://www.lexisnexis.com/academic/2upa/Aph/truman_docs/guide_intros/tru12.htm).

419. The Washington Post Writers Group, Ellen Goodman, "Forgiving History?" (at http://www.postwritersgroup.com/archives/good1212.htm).

420. Documentary History of the Truman Presidency, "The Truman Administration's Civil Rights Program: The Report of the Committee on Civil Rights and President Truman's Message to Congress of February 2, 1948" (at http://www.lexisnexis.com/academic/2upa/Aph/truman_docs/guide_intros/tru11.htm), and "The Truman Administration's Civil Rights Program: President Truman's Attempts to Put the Principles of Racial Justice into Law, 1948-1950" (at http://www.lexisnexis.com/academic/2upa/Aph/truman_docs/guide_intros/tru12.htm).

421. Democratic National Committee, "Brief History of the Democratic Party" (at http://www.democrats.org/about/history.html). The article states, "With the election of Harry Truman, Democrats *began* the fight to bring down the final barriers of race and gender" (emphasis added).

422. Democratic National Committee, "Brief History of the Democratic Party" (at http://www.democrats.org/about/history.html).

423. *The Civil Rights Act of 1964*, p. 25.

424. The White House Historical Association, "African Americans and the White House: the 1950s" (at http://www.whitehousehistory.org/05/subs/05_c17.html).

425. *The Civil Rights Act of 1964*, pp. 26-27.

426. History Matters, "The Negro Voter: Can He Elect a President?" (at http://historymatters.gmu.edu/search.php?function=print&id=6331).

427. *The Civil Rights Act of 1964*, pp. 26-27; see also *Civil Rights - 1957: Hearings Before the Subcommittee on Constitutional Rights of the Committee on the Judiciary United States Senate Eighty-Fifth Congress, First Session* (Washington, DC: Government Printing Office, 1960), pp. 125-131.

428. *The Civil Rights Act of 1964*, p. 28.

429. *The Civil Rights Act of 1964*, pp. 28-29.

430. U. S. Senate, "Filibuster and Cloture" (at http://www.senate.gov/artandhistory/history/common/briefing/Filibuster_Cloture.htm).

431. *The Civil Rights Act of 1964*, pp. 29-30.

432. *The Civil Rights Act of 1964*, pp. 26, 31.

433. *The Civil Rights Act of 1964*, p. 31.

434. *The Civil Rights Act of 1964*, p. 34.

435. *The Civil Rights Act of 1964*, p. 34.

436. *The Civil Rights Act of 1964*, p. 33.

437. *The Civil Rights Act of 1964*, pp. 36-37.

438. *The Civil Rights Act of 1964*, p. 25.

439. Alabama Department of Archives & History, "Alabama Governors: George Corley Wallace" (at http://www.archives.state.al.us/govs_list/g_wallac.html), and "Governor George C. Wallace's School House Door Speech" (at http://www.archives.state.al.us/govs_list/schooldoor.html).

440. *The Civil Rights Act of 1964*, pp. 24, 26, 30-31.

441. U. S. Senate, "1964-Present: June 10, 1964, Civil Rights Filibuster Ended" (at http://www.senate.gov/artandhistory/history/minute/Civil_Rights_Filibuster_Ended.htm).

442. *The Civil Rights Act of 1964*, p. 35; U. S. Senate "1964-Present: June 10, 1964, Civil Rights Filibuster Ended" (at http://www.senate.gov/artandhistory/history/minute/Civil_Rights_Filibuster_Ended.htm).

443. *Congressional Quarterly* (Washington, DC: Congressional Quarterly Service, 1965), Vol. 20, pp. 606, 696, 88th Congress, 2nd Session, vote on the Civil Rights Bill of 1964, February 10, 1964.

444. *Congressional Quarterly*, 88th Congress, 2nd Session, Vol. 20, pp. 606, 696, 88th Congress, 2nd Session, vote on the Civil Rights Bill of 1964, February 10, 1964.

445. *Congressional Record, 88th Congress, 1st Session* (Washington, DC: United States Government Printing Office, 1963), Vol. 109, pp. 11864-11865, June 27, 1963.

446. *Congressional Record, 88th Congress, 1st Session*, Vol. 109, pp. 11864-11865, June 27, 1963.

447. Library of Congress, "Today in History: January 23" (at http://memory.loc.gov/ammem/today/jan23.html).

448. *Congressional Quarterly* (Washington, DC: Congressional Quarterly Service, 1962), Vol. 18, pp. 630, 654, 87th Congress, 2nd Session, Senate and House votes on approving the Constitutional Amendment banning the poll tax, March 27 and August 27, 1962.

449. *Congressional Quarterly* (Washington, DC: Congressional Quarterly Service, 1962), Vol. 18, pp. 630, 654, 87th Congress, 2nd Session, Senate and House votes on approving the Constitutional Amendment banning the poll tax, March 27 and August 27, 1962.

450. *Harper v. Virginia Board of Elections*, 383 U. S. 663 (1966).

451. U. S. Department of State, "Civil Rights Act of 1964" (at http://usinfo.state.gov/usa/infousa/laws/majorlaw/civilr19.htm).

452. The Avalon Project, "Voting Rights Act of 1965; August 6, 1965" (at http://www.yale.edu/lawweb/avalon/statutes/voting_rights_1965.htm).

453. Digital History, "Voting Rights, Period: 1960s" (at http://www.digitalhistory.uh.edu/database/article_display.cfm?HHID=369).

454. Africana.com, "Voting Rights Acts of 1965" (at http://www.africana.com/Articles/tt_393.htm).

455. *Congressional Record, 43rd Congress, 2nd Session*, Vol. 3, p. 959, Rep. Joseph H. Rainey's speech on the Civil Rights Bill, February 3, 1875.

456. The Center for Voting and Democracy, "You've Got Mail: Voting Rights Myth Over the Internet" (at http://www.fairvote.org/vra/myths.htm); In These Times.com, "Voting Wrongs: Blacks won't forget how Bush got elected" (at http://www.inthesetimes.com/issue/25/04/muwakkil2504.html); Insight on the News, "Fat Lady Sings, Liberals Cry Foul" (at http://www.insightmag.com/global_user_elements/printpage.cfm?storyid=210807); Ardmoreite.com, "Internet rumor keeps surfacing to dismay of black leaders" (at http://www.ardmoreite.com/stories/120298/new_voting.shtml), etc.

457. About.com, "Urban Legends and Folklore: Will Black Voting Rights Expire in 2007?" (at http://urbanlegends.about.com/library/weekly/aa120298.htm); Congressman Jim Leach, "News From Representative James A. Leach" (at http://www.house.gov/leach/naacp.htm).

458. *The Associated Press*, November 11, 2002, "Democrats' Multiethnic 'Dream Team' Falters in Texas," David Koenig; *The New York Beacon*, November 20, 2002, "Recent Election Shows Texas isn't Ready for Minority Governor," Kevin Shay; *San Antonio Express-News*, November 7, 2002, "Democrats Asking Selves, 'What now?'; They Look to Future," Peggy Fikac.

459. Black Republican Council, "History of the Black Republican Council" (at http://www.blackrepublicancounciloftexas.com/Our_History.html).

460. Maryland State Archives, "Lieutenant Governor: Michael Steele" (at http://www.mdarchives.state.md.us/msa/mdmanual/08conoff/html/msa13921.html); Ohio Republican Party, "Leadership: Lt. Governor Jennette Bradley" (at http://www.ohiogop.org/Victory2002.asp?FormMode=Candidates&CID=8&T=Lt%2E+Governor+Jennette+Bradley).

461. Maryland State Archives, "Lieutenant Governor: Michael Steele" (at http://www.mdarchives.state.md.us/msa/mdmanual/08conoff/html/msa13921.html); Ohio Republican Party, "Leadership: Lt. Governor Jennette Bradley" (at http://www.ohiogop.org/Victory2002.asp?FormMode=Candidates&CID=8&T=Lt%2E+Governor+Jenne tte+Bradley); see also Black News Weekly, "Ga. Could Send 5 Blacks to Congress" (at http://www.blacknewsweekly.com/210.html); *The Weekly Standard*, November 7, 2002, "Things Go Right in Texas," Beth Henary (at http://www.weeklystandard.com/Content/Public/Articles/000/000/001/875ahmds.asp); etc.

462. From an interview with Congressman J.C. Watts, Jr. by Michael Fletcher, "In Search of 'New Solutions'" (at http://www.blackengineer.com/people/jcwatts.shtml).

463. Library of Congress, "A Republican Text-Book for Colored Voters" (at http://memory.loc.gov/cgi-bin/query/r?ammem/murray:@field(FLD001+75319795+):@@@REF); For similar sentiments see Douglass, *The Frederick Douglass Papers*, Vol. 4, p. 298, from a speech delivered in New Orleans, Louisiana, April 13th, 1872 (the quote reads "For Colored men the Republican party is the deck, all outside is the sea."), etc.

464. Woodson, *Negro Orators and Their Orations*, p. 505, Robert B. Elliott, Eulogy of Charles Sumner, 1874.

465. Douglass, *The Frederick Douglass Papers*, Vol. 2, p. 397, from a speech delivered at Ithaca, New York, October 14th, 1852.

466. *United States History in Christian Perspective*, Michael Lowman, George Thompson and Kurt Grussendorf, editors (Pensacola: A Beka Book, 1996), p. 218; African American Registry, "Oberlin College founded" (at http://www.aaregistry.com/african_american_history/337/Oberlin_College_founded); Oberlin College Archives, "RG 2/2 – Charles Grandison Finney 1792-1875" (at http://www.oberlin.edu/archive/holdings/finding/RG2/SG2/biography.html).

467. African American Registry, "Oberlin College founded" (at http://www.aaregistry.com/african_american_history/337/Oberlin_College_founded); Lorain Public Library System, "The Underground Railroad: The Lorain County Connection" (at http://www.lorain.lib.oh.us/history/underground_railroad/UGR_LorainCo.html).

468. Charles G. Finney, *Lectures on Revivals of Religion* (New York: Fleming H. Revell Company, 1868), Lecture XV, pp. 281-282.

469. David Ramsay, *Eulogium on Benjamin Rush* (Philadelphia: Bradford and Inskeep, 1813), p. 103.

470. Noah Webster, *Letters to a Young Gentleman Commencing His Education* (New Haven: S. Converse, 1823), pp. 18-19, Letter 1.

471. *Masterpieces of Negro Eloquence*, Alice Moore Dunbar, editor (New York: Dover Publications, Inc., 2000), pp. 246-247, Rev. Francis J. Grimke, from "Equality of Right for All Citizens, Black and White, Alike," March 7, 1909.

472. Matthias Burnet, *An Election Sermon, Preached at Hartford, on the Day of the Anniversary Election, May 12, 1803* (Hartford: Hudson & Goodwin, 1803), pp. 26-27.

Bibliography

BOOKS

Adams, James Truslow, ed. *Dictionary Of American History*. New York: Charles Scribner's Sons, 1940.

Adler, Mortimer J., ed. *Annals of America, The*. 19 vols. Chicago: Encyclopedia Britannica, 1968.

African American and American Indian Patriots of the Revolutionary War. Washington, DC: National Society Daughters of the American Revolution, 2001.

Allen, Richard. *The Life Experience and Gospel Labors of Rt. Rev. Richard Allen*. New York: Abingdon Press, 1960.

Appendix to the Congressional Globe, 42nd Congress, 2nd Session. Washington, DC: Congressional Globe Office, 1872.

Aptheker, Herbert, ed. *Documentary History of the Negro People in the United States, A*. 4 vols. New York: Citadel Press, 1990.

Bardolph, Richard. *The Negro Vanguard*. New York: Rinehart & Company, Inc., 1959.

Barnard, William. *Dixiecrats and Democrats*. University, AL: University of Alabama Press, 1974.

Biographical Directory of the American Congress 1774-1927. Washington, DC: United States Government Printing Office, 1928.

Blaine, James G. *Twenty Years of Congress: From Lincoln to Garfield*. 2 vols. Norwich: Henry Bill Publishing Company, 1886.

Blake, W. O. *The History of Slavery and the Slave Trade, Ancient and Modern*. Columbus: J. & H. Miller, 1858.

Brayton, Ellery M. *An Address upon the Election Law of South Carolina, and the Methods Employed to Suppress the Republican Vote*. Columbia: Wm. Sloane, 1889.

Burnet, Matthias. *An Election Sermon, Preached at Hartford, on the day of the Anniversary Election, May 12, 1803*. Hartford: Hudson & Goodwin, 1803.

Butterfield, Roger. *The American Past*. New York: Simon and Schuster, 1947.

Chalmers, David. *Hooded Americanism: The First Century of the Ku Klux Klan, 1865-1965*. New York: Doubleday & Company, Inc., 1965.

Calkins, Carroll C., ed. *The Story of America*. New York: The Reader's Digest Association, 1975.

Catton, Bruce. *The Centennial History of the Civil War. Vol. 1. The Coming Fury*. New York: Doubleday & Company, Inc., 1961.

Champagne, Anthony. *The Journal of Negro Education*. Vol. 42, No. 1, Winter 1973, pp. 58-63, "The Segregation Academy and the Law" by *Congressional Record, 84th Congress, 2nd Session*. Washington, DC: Government Printing Office, 1956.

Civil Rights - 1957: Hearings Before the Subcommittee on Constitutional Rights of the Committee on the Judiciary United States Senate Eighty-Fifth Congress, First Session. Washington, DC: Government Printing Office, 1960.

Cobb, Thomas R.R. *An Inquiry into the Law of Negro Slavery in the United States of America.* Vol. 1. Philadelphia: T. & J. W. Johnson & Co., 1858.

Coffin, Charles Carleton. *Drum-Beat of the Nation: The First Period of the War of the Rebellion from its Outbreak to the Close of 1862.* New York: Harper & Brothers, 1888.

Collins, Alan C. *The Story of American Pictures.* New York: Doubleday & Company, Inc, 1953.

Cook, Benjamin F. *History of the Twelfth Massachusetts Volunteers.* Boston: Twelfth Regiment Association, 1882.

Congressional Globe. 23rd-42nd Congress. Washington, DC: Congressional Globe Office, 1835-71.

Congressional Quarterly. Vol. 20. Washington, DC: Congressional Quarterly Service, 1965.

Congressional Record. 43rd-108th Congress. Washington, DC: Government Printing Office.

Constitution of the Pennsylvania Society for Promoting the Abolition of Slavery, and the Relief of Free Negroes, Unlawfuly Held in Bondage, The. Philadelphia: Joseph James, 1787.

Debates and Proceedings in the Congress of the United States. 1st-18th Congress. Washington: Gales and Seaton, 1849-56.

Douglass, Frederick. *Frederick Douglass Autobiographies: Narrative of the Life of Frederick Douglass, an American Slave.* New York: The Library of America, 1996.

Douglass, Frederick. *The Frederick Douglass Papers.* Edited by John W. Blassingame and John R. Mckivigan. 2-4 vols. New Haven: Yale University Press, 1991.

DuBois, W. E. Burghardt. *The Suppression of the African Slave-Trade to the United States of America.* New York: Social Science Press, 1954.

DuBois, W.E.Burghardt. *Black Reconstruction In America.* New York: The Free Press, 1998.

Dunbar, Alice Moore, ed. *Masterpieces of Negro Eloquence.* New York: Dover Publications, Inc., 2000.

Ebony Pictorial History of Black America. 3 vols. Nashville: The Southwestern Company, 1971.

Echoes From The South. New York: E. B. Treat & Co., 1866.

Elliot, Jonathan, ed. *The Debates of the Several State Conventions on the Adoption of the Federal Constitution.* 4 vols. Washington: Printed for the Editor, 1836.

Escott, Paul, and David Goldfield, ed. *Major Problems in the History of the American South.* Vol. 2. Boston: Houghton Mifflin, 1990.

Eubanks, W. Ralph. *Ever is a Long Time*. New York: Basic Books, 2003.

Farrand, Max, ed. *The Records of the Federal Convention of 1787*. 3 vols. New Haven: Yale University Press, 1911.

Finney, Charles G. *Lectures on Revivals of Religion*. New York: Fleming H. Revell Company, 1868.

Flower, Frank *History of the Republican Party, Embracing its Origin, Growth and Mission, Together with Appendices of Statistics and Information Required by Enlightened Politicians and Patriotic Citizens*. Springfield: Union Publishing Company, 1884.

Foner, Eric. *Reconstruction: America's Unfinished Revolution, 1863-1877*. New York: Harper & Row, 1988.

Franklin, Benjamin. *The Papers of Benjamin Franklin*. Edited by William Willcox. Vol. 20. New Haven: Yale University Press, 1976.

Freehling, William, and Craig Simpson, ed. *Secession Debated: Georgia's Showdown in 1860*. New York: Oxford University Press, 1992.

Galphin, Bruce. *The Riddle of Lester Maddox*. Atlanta: Camelot Publishing Company, 1968.

Garnet, Henry Highland. *Memorial Discourse; by Rev. Henry Highland Garnet, Delivered in the Hall of the House of Representatives, Washington City, D.C. on Sabbath, February 12, 1865*. Philadelphia: Joseph M. Wilson, 1865.

Garson, Robert. *The Democratic Party and the Politics of Sectionalism, 1941-1948*. Baton Rouge: Louisiana State University Press, 1974.

Graham, Andrew J., and Charles B. Collar, ed. *Pulpit and Rostrum: Sermons, Orations, Popular Lectures, &c., The*. New York: E. D. Barker, 1862.

Hancock, John. *The Great Question for the People! Essays on the Elective Franchise; or, Who Has the Right to Vote?* Philadelphia: Merrihew & Son, 1865.

Harper, James C. *Separate Schools for White and Colored with Equal Advantages; Mixed Schools Never!* Washington: F. & J. Rives & Geo. A. Bailey, 1872.

Hart, Albert Bushnell. *The American Nation: A History, Slavery and Abolition*. New York: Harper & Brothers Publishers, 1906.

Haskins, James. *Distinguished African American Political and Governmental Leaders*. Phoenix: Oryx Press, 1999.

Headley, J. T. *The Great Rebellion; A History of the Civil War in the United States*. 2 vols. Hartford: American Publishing Company, 1866.

Hill, J. J. *A Sketch of the 29th Regiment of Connecticut Colored Troops*. Baltimore, 1867.

Hodgman, Stephen. *The Nation's Sin and Punishment*. New York: American News Company, 1864.

Holy Bible, The.

Hoogenboom, Ari. *The Presidency of Rutherford B. Hayes.* Lawrence: University Press of Kansas, 1988.

Horn, Stanley. *Invisible Empire: The Story of the Ku Klux Klan 1866-1871.* New York: Gordon Press, 1972.

House of Representatives Mis. Doc. No. 53, "Condition of Affairs in Mississippi". 40th Congress, 3rd Session, January 6, 1869.

House of Representatives Report No. 16, "New Orleans Riots". 39th Congress, 2nd Session, February 11, 1867.

House of Representatives Ex. Doc. No. 268, "Condition of Affairs in the Southern States, Message from the President of the United States". 42nd Congress, 2nd Session, April 19, 1872.

House of Representatives Ex. Doc. No. 342, "General Orders – Reconsrtruction: Letter from the Secretary of War". 40th Congress, 2nd Session, July 18, 1868.

House of Representatives Report No. 265, "Vicksburgh Troubles". 43rd Congress, 2nd Session, February 27, 1875.

House of Representatives Mis. Doc. No. 154, "Testimony Taken by the Sub-Committee of Elections in Louisiana". Washington: Government Printing Office, 1870.

House of Representatives Report No. 16, "New Orleans Riots". 39th Congress, 2nd Session, February 11, 1867.

House of Representatives Report No. 92, "Affairs in Louisiana". 42nd Congress, 2nd Session, May 30, 1872.

House of Representatives Mis. Doc. No. 52, "Condition of Affairs in Georgia". 40th Congress, 3rd Session, February 12, 1869.

House of Representatives Report No. 2, "Affairs in Arkansas: Report by Mr. Poland". Washington: Government Printing Office, 1874.

House of Representatives Mis. Doc. No. 111, "Elections in Alabama: Affidavits of Discharge from Employment". 40th Congress, 2nd Session, March 26, 1868.

Hughes, Langston, Milton Meltzer, and C. Eric Lincoln. *A Pictorial History of Blackamericans.* New York: Crown Publishers, 1983.

Hutson, James. *Religion and the Founding of the American Republic.* Washington, DC: Library of Congress, 1998.

Jackson, Kenneth. *The Ku Klux Klan in the City 1915-1930.* Chicago: Ivan R. Dee, 1992.

Jacoway, Elizabeth, and C. Fred Williams, ed. *Understanding the Little Rock Crisis.* Fayetteville: University of Arkansas Press, 1999.

Johnson, Donald B, ed. *National Party Platforms, 1840-1976, Supplement 1980.* Champaign-Urbana: University of Illinois Press, 1982.

Johnson, Edward A. *The School History of the Negro Race in America From 1619 to 1890, with a short introduction as to the origin of the race; also a short sketch of Liberia.* Raleigh: Edwards & Broughton, 1891.

Jones, Absalom. *A Thanksgiving Sermon, Preached January 1, 1808, In St. Thomas's, or the African Episcopal Church, Philadelphia: on Account of the Abolition of the African Slave Trade.*

Journal of the House of Representatives of the United States of America. Volume 63. Washington: Government Printing Office, 1866.

Journal of the Senate of the United States of America. Washington: Government Printing Office, 1863-69.

Kaplan, Sidney. *The Black Presence in the Era of the American Revolution 1770-1800.* Washington: New York Graphic Society, LTD, 1973.

Kennedy, Stetson. *After Appomattox: How the South Won the War.* University Press of Florida: 1995.

Kingston, Mike, Sam Attlesey, and Mary G. Crawford. *Political History of Texas.* Austin: Eakin Press, 1992.

Kirshon, John W., ed. *Chronicle of America.* New York: Chronicle Publications.

Lamson, Peggy. *The Glorious Failure.* New York: W W Norton & Company, 1973.

Lanman, Charles. *Dictionary of the United States Congress, and the General Public.* Hartford: T. Belknap and H. E. Goodwin, 1868.

Loevy, Robert D., ed. *The Civil Rights Act of 1964: The Passage of the Law that Ended Racial Segregation.* Albany: State University of New York Press, 1997.

Logan, Rayford, and Michael Winston, ed. *Dictionary of American Negro Biography.* New York: WW Norton & Company, 1982.

Lossing, Benson, ed. *Harper's Encyclopaedia of United States History.* 10 vols. New York: Harper & Brothers, 1974.

Lossing, Benson, ed. *Harper's Popular Cyclopaedia of United States History.* 2 vols. New York: Harper & Brothers, 1889.

Lossing, Benson. *Our Country.* 6 vols. New York: James A. Bailey, 1895.

Lowman, Michael, George Thompson and Kurt Grussendorf, ed. *United States History in Christian Perspective.* Pensacola: A Beka Book, 1996.

Lynch, John R. *The Facts of Reconstruction.* New York: Neale Publishing Company, 1913.

Lynch, Rep. John Roy speech at the 1884 Republican National Convention.

Madison, James. *The Debates in the Federal Convention of 1787 Which Framed the Constitution of the United States of America.* Edited by Gaillard Hunt and James Brown Scott. New York: Oxford University Press, 1920.

Madison, James *The Papers of James Madison.* 10 vols. Edited by William T. Hutchinson and William M.E. Rachel. Washington: Langtree & O'Sullivan, 1840.

Malone, Dumas, ed. *Dictionary of American Biography*. Volume 18. New York: Charles Scribner's Sons, 1936.

McClellan, George. *McClellan's Own Story*. New York: Charles L. Webster & Company, 1887.

McKee, Thomas Hudson. *The National Conventions and Platforms of All Political Parties, 1789-1905*. New York: Burt Franklin, 1971.

McPherson, Edward. *The Political History of the United States of America, During the Great Rebellion*. Washington, DC: Philp & Solomons, 1865.

Michie, Peter. *General McClellan*. New York: D. Appleton and Company, 1901.

Middleton, Stephen, ed. *Black Congressmen During Reconstruction*. Westport, CT: Greenwood Press, 2002.

Nell, William. *Services of Colored Americans in the Wars of 1776 and 1812*. Boston: Robert F. Wallcut, 1852.

Nell, William. *The Colored Patriots of the American Revolution*. Boston: Robert F. Wallcut, 1855.

Official Report of the Proceedings of the Twenty-Ninth Republican National Convention. Republican National Committee: Dulany Vernay, Inc., 1968.

Ogden, Frederic. *The Poll Tax In The South*. University, AL: University of Alabama Press, 1958.

Olsen, Otto H., ed. *Reconstruction and Redemption in the South*. Baton Rouge: Louisiana State University Press, 1980.

Ploski, Harry and James Williams, ed. *Negro Almanac: A Reference Work on the African American*. Detroit: Gale Research Inc., 1989.

Porter, Dorothy. *Early Negro Writing*. Boston: Beacon Press, 1971.

Public Acts of the State of Tennessee Passed at the Extra Session of the Thirty-Third General Assembly, for the Year 1861. Nashville: E. G. Eastman & Co., 1861.

Quarles, Benjamin. *The Negro in the American Revolution*. Chapel Hill: University of North Carolina Press, 1961.

Ramsay, David. *Eulogium on Benjamin Rush*. Philadelphia: Bradford and Inskeep, 1813.

Reports of the Committees of the House of Representatives, Made During the First Session Thirty-Ninth Congress, 1865-66, The. Washington: Government Printing Office, 1866.

Report of Joint Select Committee to Inquire Into the Condition of Affairs in the Late Insurrectionary States. 13 vols. New York: AMS Press, 1968.

Republican Campaign Edition for the Million. Boston: John P. Jewett & Co., 1856.

Richardson, James D. *A Compilation of the Messages and Papers of the Presidents, 1789-1897* 10 vols. Published by Authority of Congress, 1899.

Rowland, Thomas. *George B. McClellan and Civil War History.* Kent: Kent State University Press, 1998.

Schwartz, Bernard. *Statutory History of the United States, Civil Rights.* New York: Chelsea House Publishers, 1970.

Sears, Stephen W. *George B. McClellan the Young Napoleon.* New York: Ticknor & Fields, 1988.

Sears, Stephen W. *The Civil War Papers of George B. McClellan. Selected Correspondence, 1860-1865.* New York: Ticknor & Fields, 1989.

Seip, Terry L. *The South Returns to Congress: Men, Economic Measures, and Intersectional Relationships, 1868-1879.* Baton Rouge: Louisiana State University Press, 1983.

Senate Mis. Doc. 82, Part 2, "In the Senate of the United States". 51st Congress, 1st Session. Washington: Government Printing Office. February 11, 1890.

Simkins, Francis, and Robert Woody. *South Carolina During Reconstruction.* Gloucester: Peter Smith, 1966.

Smalley, Eugene. *A Brief History of the Republican Party.* New York: John B. Alden, 1885.

Smith, Page. *Trial By Fire; A People's History of the Civil War and Reconstruction.* Vol. 5. New York: McGraw-Hill Book Company, 1982.

Statutes at Large, Treaties, and Proclamations of the United States of America. Boston: Little, Brown and Company.

Sumner, Charles. *Speech of the Hon. Charles Sumner, of Massachusetts, on the Barbarism of Slavery, Delivered in the U. S. Senate, June 4th, 1860.* San Francisco: Towne & Bacon, 1860.

Testimony Taken by the Joint Select Committee to Inquire into the Condition of Affairs in the Late Insurrectionary States. 13 vols. Washington: Government Printing Office, 1872.

Thornbrough, Emma Lou, ed. *Great Lives Observed: Booker T. Washington.* Englewood Cliffs, NJ: Prentice-Hall, Inc., 1969.

Thorpe, Francis Newton, ed. *The Federal and State Constitutions, Colonial Charters, and Other Organic Laws of the States, Territories, and Colonies.* 7 vols. Washington, DC: Government Printing Office, 1909.

Victor, Orville. *The History, Civil Political and Military, of the Southern Rebellion, From Its Incipient Stages to Its Close.* 2 vols. New York: James D. Torrey, 1861.

Washington, Booker T. *The Story of the Negro. The Rise of the Race from Slavery.* 2 vols. New York: Doubleday, Page & Company, 1909.

Washington, Booker T. *The Booker T. Washington Papers.* 14 vols. Edited by Louis Harlan and Raymond Smock. Chicago: University of Illinois Press, 1982.

Webster, Noah. *Letters to a Young Gentleman Commencing His Education: To Which is Subjoined a Brief History of The United States.* New Haven: S. Converse, 1823.

Weiss, Nancy. *Farewell to the Party of Lincoln. Black Politics in the Age of FDR*. Princeton: Princeton University Press, 1983.

Wellman, Manly Wade. *Giant In Gray. A Biography of Wade Hampton of South Carolina*. New York: Charles Scribner's Sons, 1949.

Wilson, James, and John Fiske, ed. *Appletons' Cyclopaedia of American Biography*. 6 vols. New York: D. Appleton and Company, 1888.

Wilson, Joseph T. *The Black Phalanx: African American Soldiers in the War of Independence, the War of 1812, and the Civil War*. Hartford: American Publishing Company, 1889.

Wilson, Woodrow. *A History of the American People*. 5 vols. New York: Harper & Brothers Publishers, 1902.

Woodson, Carter G. *Negro Orators and Their Orations*. Washington, DC: The Associated Pub., Inc., 1925.

Zangrando, Robert L. *The NAACP Crusade Against Lynching, 1909-1950*. Philadelphia: Temple University Press, 1980.

PERIODICALS

Cleveland Leader, The, Vol. XXIV, No. 4. (February 26, 1870).

Ervin, Clark Kent. "Guess Who's at the Heart of the Silent Majority." *Christian Science Monitor*, (August 15, 1997).

Fikac, Peggy. "Democrats Asking Selves, 'What now?'; They Look to Future." *San Antonio Express-News*, (November 7, 2002).

Frank Leslie's Illustrated Newspaper, New York, (April 30, 1870).

Harper's Weekly, July 23, 1859; November 12, 1864; February 18, 1865; April 28, 1866; August 25, 1866; September 1, 1866; May 25, 1867; October 3, 1868; November 6, 1869; October 19, 1872; August 12, 1876; October 21, 1876; September 25, 1880.

Hingham Patriot, The. Hingham, Massachusetts, (June 29, 1839).

Klarman, Michael J. "The White Primary Rulings" *Florida State University Law Review*, Vol. 29 (2001).

Koenig, David. "Democrats' Multiethnic 'Dream Team' Falters in Texas." *The Associated Press*, (November 11, 2002).

National Anti-Slavery Standard. "The South. The Rebel Perfidy in the Legislature. Colored Republicans Expelled." (September 26, 1868).

New York Tribune, "The Cipher Dispatches, Tribune Extra No. 44" (New York, 1879).

Shay, Kevin. "Recent Election Shows Texas isn't Ready for Minority Governor." *The New York Beacon*, (November 20, 2002).

West, Thomas G. "Was the American Founding Unjust? The Case of Slavery." *Principles*, (Spring/Summer 1992).

Williams, Walter E. "Some Fathers Fought Slavery." *Creators Syndicate, Inc.*, (May 26, 1993).

ORIGINAL DOCUMENTS

"The Presidential Election. Vote For General McClellan." 1864, from an original in our possession.

"The Republican Party: Its Mission to Save the Country from the Horrors of a New Rebellion." 1874, from an original in our possession.

House of Representatives, 38th Congress, 1st Session, "A Bill to Establish a Bureau of [Emancipation,] Freedmen's Affairs." 1864, from an original in our possession.

U. S. Senate Bill 145, "A Bill to equalize the pay of soldiers in the United States army." 1864, from an original in our possession.

"Amnesty Oath." E. Baton Rouge, LA. 1865, from an original in our possession.

Rebel Handbill. "Radical Members of the So. Ca. Legislature." 1868, from an original in our possession.

"Rebel Members of the 1868 Democratic National Convention." 1868, from an original in our possession.

"Tricks of the Republican Executive Committee Exposed: Ohio School System – Who are its Founders." 1875, from an original in our possession.

"Politics and the School Question: Attitude of the Republican and Democratic Parties in 1876." 1876, from an original in our possession.

"Why I Will Not Vote the Democratic Ticket." c. 1880, from an original in our possession.

"Read Laws United States!"; citing the federal law passed on May 31, 1870, entitled "An Act to Enforce the Rights of Citizens of the United States to Vote in the Several States of this Union and for other Purposes." 1880, from an original in our possession.

"Who's A Democrat!" c. 1936 campaign piece, from an original in our possession.

From an original letter written by Mrs. Caroline Johnson and sold at auction by Historical Collectible Auctions, on November 6th, 2003; a copy of the letter is in our possession.

COURT CASES

Plessy v. Ferguson, 163 U. S. 537 (1896).

Brown v. Board of Education, 347 U. S. 483 (1954).

Civil Rights Cases, 109 U. S. 3 (1883).

Dred Scott v. Sanford, 60 U. S. 393, 572-3 (1856).

Gomillion v. Lightfoot, 364 U. S. 339, 346-348 (1960).

Grovey v. Townsend, 295 U. S. 45, 55 (1935).

Harper v. Virginia Board of Elections, 383 U. S. 663 (1966).

Nixon v. Herndon, 273 U. S. 536 (1927).

South Carolina v. Katzenbach, 383 U. S. 301, 311 (1966).

Websites

Africana: Gateway to the Black World (at http://www.africana.com).

AfricanAmericans.com (at http://www.africanamericans.com).

About (at http://www.about.com).

African American Registry (at http://www.aaregistry.com).

Alabama Department of Archives and History: Alabama Moments in American History (at http://www.alabamamoments.state.al.us).

Alabama Public Television (at http://www.aptv.org).

Bartleby.com (at http://www.bartleby.com).

Biographical Directory of the United States Congress (at http://bioguide.congress.gov).

BlackVoices.com (at http://www.blackvoices.com).

Cato Institute (at http://www.cato.org).

Center for Educational Reform (at http://www.edreform.com).

Centers for Disease Control and Prevention (at http://www.cdc.gov).

CNN (at http://www.cnn.com).

Colorado College (at http://www.coloradocollege.edu).

Columbia Journalism Review (at http://www.cjr.org).

Congressional Black Caucus (at http://www.house.gov/cummings/cbc/cbchome.htm).

Democratic National Committee (at http://www.democrats.org).

Fact Monster (at http://www.factmonster.com).

Florida Center for Interactive Media (at http://www.fcim.org).

Freedmen's Bureau Online, (at http://freedmensbureau.com).

Furman University (at http://www.furman.edu).

The Gallup Organization (at http://www.gallup.com).

George Mason University (at http://www.gmu.edu).

Georgia Secretary of State (at http://www.sos.state.ga.us).

HarpWeek (at http://www.harpweek.com).

Harris Interactive (at http://www.harrisinteractive.com).

Harvard University Press (at http://www.hup.harvard.edu).

History of Jim Crow (at http://www.jimcrowhistory.org).

Infoplease (at http://www.infoplease.com).

Joint Center for Political and Economic Studies (at http://jointcenter.org).

Library of Congress (at http://www.loc.gov).

Louisiana, A History (at http://www.louisianahistory.org).

Louisiana Secretary of State (at http://www.sec.state.la.us).

Maryland State Archives (at http://www.mdarchives.state.md.us).

MyFlorida.com (at http://www.myflorida.com).

NationMaster.com (at http://www.nationmaster.com).

National Center for Education Statistics (at http://nces.ed.gov).

National Center For Policy Analysis (at http://www.ncpa.org).

National Constitution Center (at http://www.constitutioncenter.org).

National Park Service (at http://www.nps.gov).

Oberlin College (at http://www.oberlin.edu).

Office of the Clerk, U. S. House of Representatives (at http://clerk.house.gov).

Ohio Historical Society (at http://dbs.ohiohistory.org).

Ohio State University (at http://www.osu.edu).

Old Dominion University Libraries (at http://www.lib.odu.edu).

Our Georgia History (at http://www.ourgeorgiahistory.com).

PBS (at http://www.pbs.org).

Policy Review Online (at http://www.policyreview.org).

Project Gutenberg (at http://www.gutenberg.net).

Public Agenda (at http://www.publicagenda.org).

Republican National Committee (at http://www.rnc.org).

SHG Resources (at http://www.shgresources.com).

South Carolina Department of Archives and History (at http://www.state.sc.us/scdah).

Texas State Library & Archives Commission (at http://www.tsl.state.tx.us).

The Citadel (at http://www.citadel.edu).

The History Makers (at http://www.thehistorymakers.com).

The White House (at http://www.whitehouse.gov).

United States Senate (at http://www.senate.gov).

University of Georgia: GeorgiaInfo (at http://www.cviog.uga.edu/Projects/gainfo).

University of Houston: Digital History (at http://www.digitalhistory.uh.edu).

University of Missouri-Kansas City: School of Law (at http://www.law.umkc.edu).

University of Oregon (at http://www.uoregon.edu).

University of Texas at Austin: Handbook of Texas Online (at http://www.tsha.utexas.edu/handbook/online).

University of Virginia Library (at http://fisher.lib.virginia.edu).

USAToday (at http://www.usatoday.com).

U. S. Census Bureau (at http://www.census.gov).

United States Department of Justice (at http://www.usdoj.gov).

U. S. Department of State (at http://www.state.gov).

U. S. National Archives & Records Administration (at http://www.archives.gov).

White House Historical Association (at http://www.whitehousehistory.org).

World Book (at http://www.worldbook.com).

Yale University: The Avalon Project (at http://www.yale.edu/lawweb/avalon).

Zogby International (at http://www.zogby.com).

Index

~ Symbols ~

101st Airborne Division 90
12th Massachusetts 32
13th Amendment
vote on 37–38
14th Amendment
Democrats seek repeal of 111
vote on 52
15th Amendment
and African American voting rights
131
Democrats seek repeal of 111–112
vote on 68–69
15th Street Presbyterian Church (DC)
41, 136
1876 Presidential Election 80–81,
83–85
1957 Civil Rights Bill 127
1964 Civil Rights Act 129, 130
1965 Voting Rights Act 129, 130–131
24th Amendment 130–131
29th Connecticut Regiment
Pres. Lincoln visit 33–35

~ A ~

Abortion
and African Americans 24
Adams, Pres. John
anti-slavery leader 7
Adams, Pres. John Quincy
on slavery 17
Adams, Samuel
anti-slavery leader 7
African Americans
and abortion 24
and Christian faith 36
and educational choice 93
and lynchings 119

Alabama
and black voter suppression 110
and literacy tests 104
and property ownership requirements 109–110
and revision of State constitutions
109
first black legislators 45
slave population 26
Allen, Rev. Richard
and Christian spirit 118–119
and St. Thomas' Church 15
worked with Benjamin Rush 135
Almond, Gov. James 91
American Revolution
black soldiers fighting in 5
AME denomination 15, 118
Arkansas
and white-only primaries 107
State constitution rewritten 58
Arkansas National Guard 89
Armistead, James 5
Arnold, Benedict 75

~ B ~

"Black Cabinet" 121
"Bleeding Kansas" 20
Bethel Church 15
Bible
Democrats pictured burning 103
quoted by Absalom Jones 15
quoted by Douglass 134
quoted by Noah Webster 136
stories about David 7
Bilbo, Sen. Theodore 123
Birmingham
and black voter suppression 110
and Pres. Kennedy 128
Birth of a Nation 112

Black Codes 105–106
Breckenridge, John C. 25
Bridges, Ruby 91
Brooke, Sen. Edward
   and the 1968 Republican National
      Convention 95
   elected in a statewide election 66
Brooks, Rep. Preston
   attacked Charles Sumner 21
Brown v. Board of Education 88
Bruce, Sen. Blanche Kelso 66
Buchanan, James 22
Burke, Yvonne Brathwaite 95
Burnet, Rev. Matthias 137
Byrd, Sen. Robert 129–130

~ C ~

Cain, Rep. Richard
   on Black Codes 106
   on Democrats' opposition to African
      Americans 119
   speech against descrimination
      73–75
Canada
   African Americans fled to 19
Capitol building
   church service in 39–40
Celler, Rep. Emanuel 128
Chandler, Gov. Happy 92
Christianity
   and forgiveness 118
   injunctions of 134
Christians 135
Civil Rights Commission
   created by Pres. Eisenhower 127
   Pres. Kennedy bases bill upon find-
      ings of 129
   proposed by Pres. Truman 123
Civil Rights Division 127
Clement, Gov. Frank 92
Cleveland, Pres. Grover
   elected 110
   removal of Frederick Douglass 10

Cockran, Rep. Bourke 111
Coleman, Gov. James 89–90
Collins, Gov. LeRoy 92
Colorado
   part of the Kansas-Nebraska Terri-
      tory 20
*Colored Patriots of the AmericanRevolu-
      tion* 6
Confederacy
   formation of 25
Confederate battle flag
   Harper's Weekly illustration 99
   true heritage of 92
Conkling, Sen. Roscoe 67
Constitution, U.S.
   13th Amendment added 37
   14th Amendment added 53
   15th Amendment added 68–69
   24th Amendment added 130
   amendments ignored by Democrats 58
   and the Fugitive Slave Law 18
   an anti-slavery document 10–11, 13
   color washed out of 68
   Democrats claim Amendments "null
      and void" 111
   Democrats not bound by Amend-
      ments 103
   how amended 37–38
   laws passed violating 105
   mentioned by Frederick Douglass 110
   mentioned by Rep. Elliott 75
   mentioned by Rep. Rainey 120
   mentioned by Rev. Garnet 41
   mentioned by Stephens 30
   selection of Senators under 66
   Three-Fifths Clause 9, 11–13
Cromwell, Oliver 5

~ D ~

Davis, Gov. Jimmie 91
Davis, Jefferson
   President of the Confederacy 26
   replaced by Revels 63

Declaration of Independence
  compared with the Emancipation
    Proclamation 97
  JQA quotes 18
  mentioned by Rep. Elliott 78, 134
  mentioned by Rev. Grimke 137
  Republican platform based upon 22
  signed by Benjamin Rush 15, 135
  signers of 7–8
Delaware
  and poll tax 103
Democratic National Committee
  website 14, 124–125
Democratic National Convention
  1868 53, 56
  1948 123
  1972 95
Democratic Party
  1856 Platform 23
  1860 Platform 23
  1868 Platform 56
  and Civil Rights 110–111
  and education 86–91
  and educational choice 93
  and free speech for churches 42
  and human life 24
  and lynchings 115
  and marriage 43
  and poll taxes 130
  and Rebels 53
  and Rep. Josiah Walls 85
  and repeal of the 14th and 15th
    Amendments 111
  and Southern Redemption 100–103
  and Ten Commandments displays 42
  and the 13th Amendment 37
  and the 14th Amendment 53
  and the 15th Amendment 68
  and the 1875 Civil Rights bill 79
  and the 1876 election 81–82
  and the bill punishing Klan vio-
    lence 73
  and the Civil Rights Act of 1964 and
    Voting Rights Act of 1965 129
  and the Freedmen's Bureau 56
  and the Klan 50–51, 122
  and voluntary prayer 42
  difference between Northern and
    Southern 25
  first black Democratic Congress-
    man 67
  majority party in Congress 17
  rebuttal against Rep. Elliott 78
  split in 1860 24
De Large, Rep. Robert 61
Dirksen, Sen. Everett 129
Dixiecrat Party 123
Dixon, Thomas Jr. 112
Douglas, Sen. Stephen 23, 25
Douglass, Frederick 9, 133
  and righteousness 134
  on civil rights progress 33
  on Democrats 110–111
  on Democrats' opposition to African
    Americans 120
  on the Constitution 10–11
  on the Emancipation Proclamation
    28–29
Dred Scott decision 23–24
Duke, David 122
Dyer, Rep. Leonidas 115
Dyer Anti-Lynching Bill 115

~ E ~

Eastland, Sen. James 127–128
Eisenhower, Pres. Dwight D.
  and Civil Rights 126–128
  and desegregation 89–90
Elliott, Rep. Robert Brown
  accomplishments of 62
  and principles 133–134
  on Black Codes 105–106
  on the purpose of the Democratic
    Party 108

rebuttal against Rep. Stephens 74–77
speech on Klan violence 70–72
Emancipationists 21
Emancipation Proclamation 28, 97

~ F ~

Faubus, Gov. Orval 89, 91–92
Ferguson, Gov. Ma 122
Finney, Rev. Charles
and politics 134–135
Firearms
blacks prevented from owning 105
Florida
and "southern conference of true
Democrats" 123–124
and black voter suppression 110
and revision of State constitutions 109
and the 1876 Presidential Election 81
and the withholding of voting
rights 109
and white-only primaries 107
first black legislators 46
State constitution rewritten 58
Flournoy, Robert
testimony of 59–60
Forrest, Nathan Bedford
and Fort Pillow 56
and the Klan 57
delegate to the 1868 Democratic
Convention 56
pictured in Harper's Weekly 103
Fort Griswold 75
Fort Pillow 57–58
Franklin, Benjamin
and first abolition society 15
anti-slavery leader 7
Free-Soilers 21
Freedmen's Bureau
1868 Democratic Platform and 56
bill establishing 29
Freeman, Jordan 75

Fremont, John C. 22
Fugitive Slave Law 18
repealed by Republicans 29

~ G ~

Garfield, Pres. James A.
and the election of 1880 96
appointment of Frederick Douglass 10
Garnet, Rev. Henry Highland 39–42
Garrison, William Lloyd
beliefs on the Constitution 10
Georgia
and segregated schools 90
and white-only primaries 107
Democrats expell elected blacks 46
first black legislators 46
readmission to the Union 64–65
State constitution rewritten 58
Gerry, Elbridge
and gerrymandering 106
anti-slavery leader 7
argued against slave-holders 12
Gerrymandering 106–107
Graham, Rev. Billy 92
Grandfather clauses 104
Grant, Pres. Ulysses S.
appointment of Frederick Douglass 10
signed Civil Rights bills 69
Greeley, Horace
on the purpose of the Democratic
Party 79
Griffin, Gov. Marvin 90
Griffith, D. W. 112
Grimke, Rev. Francis 136–137

~ H ~

Hampton, Gov. Wade
and the "Red Shirts" 54
delegate to the 1868 Democratic
Convention 54–56
Hancock, Gen. Winfield Scott 96

Harper, Rep. James 87–88
Harper's Weekly 55, 63, 82, 99
Harrison, Pres. Benjamin
  appointment of Frederick Douglass 10
Hayes, Pres. Rutherford B.
  and the 1876 election 80
  and The Great Compromise 84–85
  appointment of Frederick Douglass 10
Henry, Patrick
  quoted by Rev. Garnet 40
Hide-and-seek polling places 104
History of the American People 112
Holland, Sen. Spessard 130
Hoover, Pres. Herbert
  and the 1932 election 113
  received three-fourths of the black
    vote 121
Hopkins, Stephen
  anti-slavery leader 7
Howard University 136

~ I ~

Idaho
  part of the Kansas-Nebraska Terri-
    tory 20
Illinois
  election of African Americans 132
  entry into the Union 14
Indiana
  entry into the Union 14
Iowa
  entry into the Union 14

~ J ~

"John Brown's Body" 32
Jackson, Rev. Charles 116–117
Jefferson, Thomas
  quoted by Rev. Garnet 40
  slave-owner 7
  started the Democratic Party 14
Jim Crow laws 105–106

Johnson, Edward
  historian 7
Johnson, Lyndon Baines
  and Civil Rights 129–130
  and free speech for churches 43
Johnson, Pres. Andrew
  appointed Gov. Sharkey 59
  vetoed Civil Rights bills 68–69
Jones, Rev. Absalom
  sermon by 14–17
Jordan, Rep. Barbara 67

~ K ~

Kansas
  battles over slavery 20
Kansas-Nebraska Act 19–20
Kansas-Nebraska Territory 20–21
Kennedy, Pres. John F. 128
Kentucky
  entry into the Union 14
King, Rev. Martin Luther (Jr.) 129
Kirk, Ron 132
Knights of the Golden Circle 26, 99
Ku Klux Klan
  and *Birth of a Nation* 112
  first Grand Wizard 57
  formed by Democrats 49–50
  illustration in *Harper's Weekly* 99
  mentioned by Rep. Rapier 108
  pushcard 52
  Republicans not members of 99

~ L ~

Lincoln, Pres. Abraham
  1860 election 23, 25
  and Carolyn Johnson 36–37
  and the 13th Amendment 37
  and the Emancipation Proclama-
    tion 28
  replaced General McClellan 31
  visits Richmond 36

Lincoln University 136
Literacy tests 103–104
Long, Rep. Jefferson 62
Louisiana
  and revision of State constitutions 109
  and the 1876 Presidential Election 81
  and white-only primaries 107
  first black legislators 45
  slave population 26
  State constitution rewritten 58
Louisville Courier-Journal 100
Lynch, Rep. John Roy
  accomplishments of 94–95
  and the 1884 Republican National
    Convention 95
  on Democrats' opposition to African
    Americans 119
  on Democrats' voter fraud 82–83
  on education 88
  on his love of Country 94–95
  on opposition to civil rights 100
  on passage of the 1875 Civil Rights
    bill 79
Lynchings 115–116

~ M ~

"Multiple ballots" 104
Maddox, Gov. Lester 91
Martin, Luther
  argued against slave-holders 12
  on representation 12
Maryland
  election of African Americans 132
Massachusetts
  broadside warning 18–19
McClellan, Gen. George
  1864 campaign piece 32
  failures of 31–32
McEnery, Sen. Samuel 111–112
McKinley, Pres. William 112
Michigan
  entry into the Union 14

Minnesota
  entry into the Union 14
Mississippi
  and black voter suppression 110
  and Governor Coleman 89
  and revision of State constitutions
    59, 109
  and white-only primaries 107
  first black legislators 45
  population of 60
  slave population 26
  voter registration 131
Missouri Compromise 17
Montana
  part of the Kansas-Nebraska Terri-
    tory 20
Morgan, Sen. John Tyler 111
Morris, Gouverneur
  on representation 11
Morrow, Frederic 126
Moseley-Braun, Sen. Carol 66, 132

~ N ~

"Negro supremacy" 56
NAACP 115, 131, 136
Nebraska
  part of the Kansas-Nebraska Terri-
    tory 20
Nell, William 6, 7
New Orleans
  and Ruby Bridges 91
  Republican Convention attacked
    48–49
Northwest Ordinance 13
North Carolina
  and poll tax 103
  and revision of State constitutions
    58, 109
  first black legislators 46
  slave State formed from 14
North Dakota
  part of the Kansas-Nebraska Terri-
    tory 20

~ O ~

Oath of Loyalty 44
Obama, Sen. Barack 66
Ohio
  election of African Americans 132
  entry into the Union 14

~ P ~

Phillips, Wendell 68
Pilgrims
  and slaves 6
Pinchback, Lt.Gov. P. B. S. 48
Pleasant Grove Missionary Baptist
        Church 116
Plessey v. Ferguson 111
"Politics and the School Question:
        Attitude of the Republican and
        Democratic Parties in 1876" 86
Poll tax 103, 130–131
Princeton Theological Seminary 136
Puritans
  and slaves 6

~ Q ~

Quarles, Benjamin
  historian 7

~ R ~

"Radicals" 52
"Rebels" 26
"Red Shirts" 54
Rainey, Rep. Joseph Hayne
  accomplishments of 62
  first African American Congress-
        man 66
  on Democrats 109
  on Democrats' opposition to African
        Americans 120–121
  on education 88
  on voting 131
  speech on Klan violence 71–72

story of Sen. Winsmith 50–51
Rapier, Rep. James T.
  on the Klan 108
Reparations 113–114
Republican National Convention
  1884 95
  1968 95
  2000 95
Republican Party
  1860 Platform 23
  1864 Platform 33
  abolished slavery in DC 27
  and education 86–91
  and free speech for churches 43
  and lynchings 115
  and marriage 43
  and poll taxes 130
  and Ten Commandments displays 43
  and the 13th Amendment 37
  and the 14th Amendment 53
  and the 15th Amendment 68
  and the 1875 Civil Rights bill 79
  and the Civil Rights Act of 1964
        and the Voting Rights Act of
        1965 130
  and voluntary prayer 42
  first platform 22–23
  formation of 21
  passed Civil Rights bills 68–69
Republican Party of Texas
  formation of 44
Revels, Sen. Hiram Rhodes
  accomplishments of 61
  Democrats fight seating of 62
  on Georgia's readmission 65–66
Rock, John 43–44
Roosevelt, Pres. Franklin Delano
  and Civil Rights 113
  Black Cabinet 121
Roosevelt, Pres. Teddy
  invited Booker T. Washington to the
        White House 112

Rush, Benjamin
  and party affiliation 135–136
  and St. Thomas' Church 14
  anti-slavery leader 7
Russell, Sen. Richard 90, 129

~ S ~

"Segregation Academies" 91
"Separate Schools for Whites and
        Colored with Equal Advantag-
        es; Mixed Schools Never!" 87
"Solid Democratic South" 85
"Southern conference of true Demo-
        crats" 123–124
"Southern Manifesto" 89
"Southern Redemption" 100–103, 112
"States' Rights" 27–28, 92
Salem, Peter 5
Second Great Awakening 134
Seibels, E. W. 50
Selma, Alabama 110
Services of Colored Americans 6
Sharkey, Gov. William 59
Sherman, Roger
  anti-slavery leader 7
Shivers, Gov. Allan 89
Slavery
  abolished 37
  Democrats maintain and promote
        17–18
  first slaves 6, 9
Slave trade
  abolished 14
Smith, Col. French 60
Smith, Rep. Howard 128
Smoke, Charles 115
Smoke, Richard 115
South Carolina
  and revision of State constitutions
        58, 109
  and the 1876 Presidential Election 81

and white-only primaries 107
  first black legislators 45
  Klan pushcard 52
  number of slave inhabitants 11
  slave population 26
South Dakota
  part of the Kansas-Nebraska Terri-
        tory 20
St. Philips Church 87
St. Thomas' Church 14–15
Stars and Bars
  Harper's Weekly illustration 99
  true heritage of 92
Stephens, Rep. Alexander
  leader against civil rights 74
  speech on slavery 29
  Vice-President of the Confederacy 26
Sumner, Sen. Charles
  and John Rock 43
  anti-slavery leader 21–22
Supreme Court
  and 1875 Civil Rights laws 93
  and gerrymandering 67–68
  and poll taxes 130
  and white-only primaries 107–108
  Brown v. Board of Education 88
  Dred Scott decision 23
  Plessey v. Ferguson 111

~ T ~

"The Great Compromise" 85–86
Taft, Pres. William 112
Talmadge, Gov. Herman 89
Tennessee
  and poll tax 103
  and racial segregation 106
  and revision of State constitutions 58
  entry into the Union 14
Terrell, A. W. 111
Texas
  and black voter suppression 110
  and gerrymandering 107–108

and poll tax 103
and revision of State constitutions
    58, 109
and white-only primaries 107
election of African Americans
    132, 133
first black legislators 45
formation of Republican Party 44
The Clansman 112
Thurmond, Sen. Strom 123, 127
Tilden, Samuel
    and bribery 83
    and the election of 1876 80
Tillman, Sen. Ben 111
Timmerman, Gov. George 92
Truman, Pres. Harry S.
    and Civil Rights 123–125
    desegregated the military 121
Turner, Rep. Benjamin 61

~ U ~

Underground Railroad 19, 134

~ V ~

Virginia
    and revision of State constitutions
        58, 109
    first black legislators 46
    slave State formed from 14

~ W ~

"Who's a Democrat" 113–114
"Why I Will not Vote the Democratic
    Ticket" 97–100
Wallace, Gov. George 122
Walls, Rep. Josiah
    accomplishments of 62
    credentials challenged 85–86
Washington, Booker T.
    historian 7
    invited to White House 112

Washington, D. C.
    schools 93–94
    services in Capitol building 39–40
Watts, Rep. J. C.
    and the 2000 Republican National
        Convention 95
    elected in a non-minority district 133
Webster, Col. Fletcher 32
Webster, Noah
    on voting 136
Whigs 21
Whipple, Prince 5
White, Gov. Hugh 91
White-only primaries 107–108
White supremacy
    Democrats and 30
Wilson, James
    anti-slavery leader 7
    argued against slave-holders 12
Wilson, Joseph
    historian 7
Wilson, Pres. Woodrow 112
Wisconsin 14
Witherspoon, John
    anti-slavery leader 7
Woodson, Carter
    historian 7
Wyoming
    part of the Kansas-Nebraska Terri-
        tory 20

~ X ~

~ Y ~

Young, Rep. Andrew 67

~ Z ~

Zion Methodist Church 9

Also Available from WallBuilders

A history curriculum that unabashedly delivers the truth!
Drive Through History America
written by David Barton & presented by award-winning actor Dave Stotts

Visit our website for other great resources!

800-873-2845 • www.wallbuilders.com